# HOW TO BE A MAN

## DISCOVERING
## WHAT IT MEANS TO
## BE A DISCIPLE

ARE YOU WILLING TO TAKE THE

# HOW TO BE A MAN

## CHALLENGE

We've crafted a pretty cool experience to go alongside this book. Now, you can do this book on its own and not miss a thing. But if you'd like to take your experience to the next level, we've created the "How To Be A Man Challenge." The challenge equips you to get the absolute most out of this book.

**IF YOU'RE A DAD, THE CHALLENGE WILL HELP YOU AND YOUR SON GROW CLOSER TO CHRIST TOGETHER.**

**IF YOU ARE A GUY IN A SMALL GROUP WITH OTHER MEN, THE CHALLENGE WILL HELP YOU COLLECTIVELY BECOME THE MEN GOD IS CALLING YOU TO BE.**

**IF YOU'RE A YOUTH WORKER DISCIPLING TEENAGERS, THE CHALLENGE WILL HELP YOU LEAD THESE GUYS TO PURSUE CHRIST-CENTERED MASCULINITY.**

**AND IF YOU'RE JUST A MAN READING THIS BOOK ON YOUR OWN, THE CHALLENGE WILL GIVE YOU A WAY TO REFLECT ON WHAT YOU'RE LEARNING AND PUT IT INTO ACTION.**

Sure, you can do this without taking the challenge. But don't you want to go bigger? Man up. Take the challenge.

**GO TO HOWTOBEAMANCHALLENGE.COM**

## HOW TO BE A MAN: DISCOVERING WHAT IT MEANS TO BE A DISCIPLE

Published by Iron Hill Press in the United States of America.

ISBN 10: 9781935832942

# HOW TO BE A MAN

DISCOVERING WHAT IT MEANS TO BE A DISCIPLE

# TABLE OF CONTENTS

_____

_____

_____

_____

_____

# INTRODUCTION

Have you ever had that moment in the middle of a conversation where you suddenly realize that you and the individual you're speaking with aren't on the same page? Maybe you're telling a story about a person, and they think you're talking about someone else until a critical detail is shared. Perhaps you're describing a restaurant you both love until one of you realizes you've never actually been to the place you're talking about. Maybe it was a meeting you and a friend both believed you attended, until a specific point where one of you realizes you must not have been there after all. It can be a confusing moment.

Isn't it interesting that two people can think they're talking about the same thing only to find out that they aren't? Unfortunately, when it comes to discipleship, it's a pretty common occurrence.

Discipleship. If you're a man who has spent any time in church, and I hope you have, you've heard the word. Discipleship. We toss it around a lot, but at the end of the day, do men understand what it means? What is a disciple? What does discipleship really look like?

The word "discipleship" means different things to different people. For instance, when you mention discipleship to a church leader, they might think about programs where people gather at specific times, eat donuts, drink coffee, and study the Bible. "Yeah, discipleship. That's Sunday School." While this answer isn't necessarily wrong (Sunday School or small groups can be an important aspect of discipleship), it's incredibly insufficient. Discipleship isn't merely the programs at your church.

For others, discipleship brings to mind an image of meeting one-on-one with someone, learning from them about what it means to go deeper in your faith. This type of mentoring relationship can be an important aspect of discipleship. But again, if this is what you think of when you hear the word, it's not a broad enough definition.

The purpose of this book is to help men know what the word discipleship means. To be a disciple is to be a follower. Period. And so discipleship is followership. Discipleship is the journey, the process, that every Christian undergoes to be a more devoted follower of Christ. Discipleship is Jesus' call on all who would believe in Him. In Luke 9:23-24, Jesus said, "[23] Whoever wants to be my disciple must deny themselves and take up their cross daily and follow me. [24] For whoever wants to save their life will lose it, but whoever loses their life for me will save it" (NIV). Discipleship is the natural result of genuinely committing to a life surrendered to Jesus.

Discipleship is not the exception. There aren't two levels of Christians: Christians and disciples. Discipleship is God's expectation of everyone who enters into a relationship with Him. It's not an exclusive club for the extra devout, which is an essential truth to process. Because if that's true (which it is), it means you have to KNOW what it means to be a disciple. You have to know what God expects of you.

That's where this book comes in.

This is the third book in the *How To Be A Man* series. The response to the first two books has been, to put it quite plainly, overwhelming. I wish I had time to share with you the stories we continue to hear about what God is doing in men's lives through these books. God is awakening men to the vital role they play in the lives of their family, their churches, and their communities. But for many men, there remains a significant hurdle: They know they are called to discipleship, but they don't know what a disciple looks like.

The purpose of this book is to show men, many for the first time, a picture of a disciple. After spending significant time and energy studying what the Bible has to say about discipleship, we've identified eight characteristics of disciples. Together, these characteristics paint a holistic picture of what it looks like to be a man who is authentically pursuing Jesus. The eight attributes of discipleship are:

- Disciples have been transformed by Christ.
- Disciples surrender to a Gospel-centered life.
- Disciples hunger to know God.
- Disciples desire to worship God.
- Disciples pursue personal holiness.
- Disciples embrace Christian community.
- Disciples engage with their surroundings.
- Disciples invest in multiplying disciples.

How does this picture sit with you? When you evaluate your life against this description of a disciple, how do you match up? Are some of these characteristics evident in your life? Are others lacking? Our purpose for painting this picture is to give you a clear picture of what a disciple looks like. You can't hit a target if you don't know what you're aiming at. But the only problem is that once you know what the goal is, you're accountable for how you go after it.

The purpose of this book is to both equip and challenge you to become an authentic follower of Christ. The men who contributed to this book don't have all the answers. None are perfect. But I know these men personally, and I can tell you that they are deeply committed to their faith. Over the 40 days of devotions in this book, the pathway of discipleship is clearly laid out. As a man seeking to follow Jesus more faithfully, your task is to let these truths speak into your life. God WANTS you to follow Him and His Holy Spirit helps you to do so. Your call is to surrender your will to God, allow Him to change you, and lead out in a deepening commitment to Him.

As you begin this book, let me challenge you not to do so lightly. The stakes are too high for you to be yet another man who has a faith defined by passivity and ambivalence. The world needs godly men engaging with culture, being bold witnesses, and living as salt and light.

My prayer, and the prayer of everyone here at Iron Hill Press, is that this book will be a catalyst for taking your faith to the next level. We hope that God works through these words to lead you to a more authentic pursuit of Him.

Andy Blanks
Co-founder/Publisher, Iron Hill Press

# WEEK 1:

# DISCIPLES HAVE BEEN TRANSFORMED BY CHRIST

I love barbeque. But before I can lay into a pulled-pork street taco, I have to choose the perfect pork shoulder from the butcher.

Maybe you're reading this in your home. Your home didn't just happen. It started with blueprints that guided the build-out process.

Think about a professional athlete. They didn't just arrive. At some point, long ago, they picked up a ball and began to learn the game.

Discipleship is no different. Before we can learn what it means to be a disciple, we have to start at the beginning.

What is the most fundamental aspect of discipleship? Before we can even consider what discipleship looks like, we have to be transformed by a saving relationship with Christ. Discipleship starts with salvation through Jesus' work on the cross. Jesus lived a sinless life and died as an atoning sacrifice for our sins to rescue humanity from the death that sin rightly earns for us (2 Corinthians 5:21 and Romans 6:23). When we accept Jesus' payment on our behalf by grace through faith, we are transformed (2 Corinthians 5:17).

Don't miss that word. "Transformed." You see, we're not just better versions of ourselves. We're something entirely new. And this "newness" is something we need to explore before we jump into defining what it means to be a disciple. That's what we're going to spend this first week doing.

Let me say a word about this transformed life: This new life is lived by the power of the Holy Spirit in us. It's not lived solely under our effort. And we can't do enough or work hard enough to be good enough. However, Scripture is clear that a transformed life looks a certain way. And we are called to bend our wills and shape our lives to follow Christ in the manner outlined in Scripture. The way we live this out is through our discipleship. In this first week, Andy Blanks helps us understand what true transformation looks like.

# WEEK I DAY I

We think we have a good idea of what a transformation is. We see an old, rusty, beater of a car refurbished, and we say it's been transformed. We see someone lose a lot of weight on a TV show, and we say they have been transformed. Maybe we watch one of the many home improvement shows on TV as the host cheerily reveals the home's transformation to the surprised homeowners. It's not that these aren't transformation. It's just that they are not transformed in the biblical sense of the word.

Read Romans 6:1-4. Here, Paul is reacting to an argument some of his opponents were making. They were essentially saying, "if God gives us grace when we sin, then the more we sin, the more grace we get." You don't have to be a biblical scholar to recognize the absurdity of this statement. Paul refuted this argument by appealing to our identities. He said in verse 2 that if we have come to saving faith in Christ, we have died to sin. Sin no longer has mastery over us; as Christ-followers, we are to hate sin. Paul then goes on to paint a powerful picture of transformation in verses 3-4.

Here, Paul makes a profound point. He uses the picture of baptism to describe the transformation we experience when we come to faith in Christ. He says that when a person goes under the water, it's as if they were buried with Jesus and that when a person comes up from the water, it's as if they were raised from the dead. But it's the phrase at the end of verse 4 that should get our attention.

Paul says that anyone who has come to faith in Jesus has been reborn, freed to "walk in newness of life." Of all people, Paul understood this. It's why he can say we're "new creations" in Christ (2 Cor. 5:17) and that our old selves were "crucified" with Jesus (Gal. 2:20). Paul understood that being a Christian means the death of our old self and the birth of something new. This is what it means to be transformed.

Men, embracing the transformation that occurs when we come to saving faith in Jesus is the foundation of what it means to be a disciple. We will never grow into faithful followers unless we embrace the new life Jesus bought for us. We can't live an "old life" faith. We must see clearly who we are in Christ, and with eyes wide open, press forward into the new purpose and vision Jesus has called us to.

# DISCIPLE-SHAPING QUESTIONS

1. Many men have come to faith in Christ but seem to live as if Jesus hasn't made much of a difference in who they are. If we know Jesus transforms us into a new creation, how do you explain Christian men who do not live as if this were true?

2. Describe the most significant difference in your life before and after you embraced the transformation Jesus has brought about in you.

3. Because the point, "Disciples have been transformed by Christ," is foundational, take some time and describe how the transformation Jesus has worked in you has impacted your life and the lives of people around you.

4. Spend some time in prayer thanking Jesus for the transformation only He can bring. Thank Him that you are a new creation and that He has led you to a place where He is using you to advance His Kingdom. Finish by asking Him to help you be more aware of the areas in your life that reflect more of your old self than the new.

# WEEK I DAY 2

SCRIPTURE PASSAGE: EPHESIANS 4:17-24

Think of the first professional athlete that comes to mind. What are his attributes? How would you describe him? Paul spends a large portion of Ephesians 4 explaining what a life with Jesus and a life without Jesus look like. And just like you can tell a professional athlete by their attributes, you can tell a true disciple by his.

Read Ephesians 4:17-24. Today and tomorrow, we're going to look at Paul's comparison of an untransformed life with a transformed one. Paul is writing to his friends in the church in Ephesus. Paul says to the Ephesians that since they have been transformed by saving faith in Jesus, their lives must be different than the Gentiles who don't know the Lord. Those who don't know the Lord, Paul says, have some distinguishing characteristics·
- Their thinking is futile, and their understanding unclear.
- They are ignorant of the truth of God.
- Their hearts are hardened to the presence of God.
- They pursue pleasure and material comfort with no regard to whether their actions are honorable.

In vs. 20, Paul writes that there can be absolutely NONE of these characteristics in the life of someone who knows Jesus. In verse 22, Paul challenges his readers to adopt a simple approach: just as if you'd take off a jacket when walking indoors, take off this old way of life. Isn't that a simple image? Just take it off! Drop it! Leave your old life behind you like dropping an old coat on the floor. In its place, we're to put on our new self. Like taking one coat off and putting another on, we're to dress ourselves to face the world as a transformed disciple of Christ.

Men, the reason transformation is so critical to discipleship is that our old way of life is "corrupt" (to use Paul's word). We cannot faithfully seek after God as a follower if we're living out of an old, dead way of operating. On the contrary, Paul says the new life that Jesus made possible for us is created to look like Jesus. This is our inheritance as children of God.

To be a follower of Christ, we have to rely on the Spirit, but that doesn't mean we don't have any responsibility. We have the responsibility to act. We have a choice. We can allow the dirty, stained, worn-out coat of our old life to still hang in our closets, where we will occasionally put it on. Or, we can throw it out, once and for all turning our backs to a life of seeking our desires and not God's. The choice is up to you. Jesus paid for a new life that imitates His own. The question is, what life are you "putting on" right now?

To be a disciple is to intentionally pursue Jesus above all else. What are you pursuing?

# DISCIPLE-SHAPING QUESTIONS

1. If you had to name one major hurdle keeping you from a more authentic followership of Jesus, what would it be?

2. Putting on the "new self" is Paul's way of describing discipleship. It's imitating Jesus in our daily lives. Think of three or four times this week when someone in your life would have recognized something you did as a Christ-like act. How can an awareness of our Christ-like actions lead us to an even greater commitment to pattern our life after Jesus?

3. How is your heart when it comes to listening and obeying God? Is it a pliable heart, one that hears and accepts God's influence? Or is it a hard heart, a stubborn heart that charges down the path of your choosing?

4. We've said the last two days that a transformed life is yours if you have come to saving faith in Jesus. But many men reading this aren't living out a transformed life. For many men, it's because they have a hard heart. If your heart is hardened to God, get on your knees now and pray to God that He would break it. Trust Him that He will. Ask Him to lead you to a place where you are willing to listen and follow.

# WEEK 1 DAY 3

SCRIPTURE PASSAGE: EPHESIANS 4:25-32

I am a runner. I laugh because God gave me a love of running, but not necessarily the physique of a runner. (Hey, big boys run, too!) I especially love trail running. I've run a ton of short trail races and a handful of marathon and ultra-marathon races. Running a long-distance race isn't easy, but it's not impossible. The secret is building up to it. It requires a lot of effort and discomfort to achieve. But when you cross the finish line, all the hard work is worth it.

Read Ephesians 4:25-32. This is the second day where you will look at Ephesians 4. In this passage, Paul makes a list of what it looks like for a disciple to embrace the transformed life. He starts with a biggie in vs. 25: truthfulness. There is a reason Jesus called Satan the "father of lies" (John 8:44). When we lie, we are aligning ourselves with Satan's values. A man seeking to be a follower of Jesus doesn't lie. A man seeking to be a follower also doesn't lose control of his temper. Anger is a normal reaction in people. But we can be angry and not sin. A disciple controls his anger, especially with those closest to him.

Paul understood honest work. He worked as a tentmaker to support his ministry work, and he worked hard (2 Thess. 3:8). In vs. 28, Paul shows us the purpose of honest work: to be generous with what we earn. In vs. 29, Paul speaks to the language of a disciple. The ONLY words that come out of our mouth should be words that lift up others. For many men, this verse is a healthy dose of conviction. But we should never shrink from the standard God sets before us. In verses 31-32, Paul encourages us to be kind and gracious with others, forgiving them, just as Jesus has done for us.

Does this list overwhelm you? It overwhelms me. I see many things on that list that I fall short of. But I'm glad it's overwhelming. I'm thankful it's a tall task. Because if it weren't, it wouldn't be worth pursuing. If God gave me a picture of what it looks like to follow Him, and it was a standard I could easily grasp under my power, it wouldn't be much of a standard. It's like running a long race. If it were easy, everyone would do it. Our faith requires that we give a lot of ourselves. But the payoff is always worth it.

As men, we should be THANKFUL that God expects so much from us. Why? Because that means that we get to journey together with Him, leaning on the Spirit for help and striving

# DISCIPLE-SHAPING QUESTIONS

1. What in Paul's list gave you the most pause? Better question: What are you going to do about it? You have a choice: you can either ignore the Spirit's conviction or act on it. Challenge yourself to listen and obey God's leading. If there is something in that list that is difficult for you, then put the work in. Address it head-on.

2. When I read this list, I am left with a feeling about what a disciple looks like. Think about this list as a whole. In your own words, describe a person who faithfully lives out these attributes.

3. Do you see yourself in the description you just wrote? If you can't answer, yes, it's OK. It just means that you and God have work to do. We are all on a journey toward faithful followership. God is never through with you. He wants you to follow Him faithfully. Spend some time in prayer today, asking God to reveal areas in your life that need refining. Ask Him for the strength to follow through on becoming more like Him. Trust that He is with you and for you.

# WEEK I DAY 4

Can I confess something to you? As a father, I can sometimes lose sight of the big picture. I can be unrealistic in my expectations of my children. Maybe it's the Marine in me, but if I'm not careful, I can communicate to them that I expect perfection. When they fall short, I can be quick to let them know. One of the many reasons I am thankful for my wonderful wife is that she knows this tendency. She is equally quick to remind me to take a step back and see the big picture: they are kids. They aren't perfect. They make mistakes, and mistakes are a part of learning.

Read 2 Peter 1:3-11. If you're like me, you need to read it through a couple of times. With lots of complex sentences, this kind of passage is very common in the introduction of letters written during Peter's day. Let's break it down a few verses at a time and get to the heart of what Peter was saying.

In verses 3-4, Peter says that in His great grace, God has allowed us to know Him and to grow in this knowledge. The reason He has allowed us to know Him is for our transformation (what we've been talking about this week). We know God, which leads to belief, which leads to transformation. That's the whole "partakers of his divine nature." When we come to faith in Jesus, we become new creations, made holy by the work Jesus did on the cross.

In verses 5-7, Peter gets to the heart of it. He says that it's not enough to simply be saved. Transformation is just the starting point. Our call is to get to work "supplementing" our faith, growing in godliness. That's the list he gives. He's saying what we've been saying all week: transformation is the foundation upon which we build our discipleship. Vs. 8 holds the real kicker for us: unless we grow in our discipleship, we're ineffective for the Kingdom.

This is why we kicked off this book with this section. So many men have come to saving faith in Jesus, but they aren't growing. They aren't becoming more Christ-like. They are not pursuing discipleship. Peter warns us of this. He says that if this describes us, we're "so nearsighted that [we are] blind." The man who isn't pursuing Jesus has lost sight of the bigger picture. What is this bigger picture? That Jesus didn't die on the cross only to save you from eternal separation from God. He also died on the cross to save you to a life of profound meaning and impact. That life of impact starts when you take discipleship seriously. That's the bigger picture. You are God's man. You are God's plan to impact the world in His name. But it won't happen unless you get serious about your faith.

# DISCIPLE-SHAPING QUESTIONS

1. Why is it easy for us to lose sight of the big picture of our faith?

2. Peter talks about the relationship between growth and effectiveness. How have you seen this in your own life? Think of someone who is super effective for the Kingdom. What do you know about their faith life? How can you model your spiritual growth on the example they've set?

3. In what ways have you experienced growth in your faith? Are you in a season of growth or drought? What changes do you need to make to ensure you are growing in your faith?

4. Spend some time in prayer asking God to help you have the strength and conviction to take your spiritual growth seriously. Ask Him for the Holy Spirit to empower and encourage your growth as you become more like Christ.

# WEEK I DAY 5

SCRIPTURE PASSAGE: 1 JOHN 3:1-3

Have you ever heard of the goal-gradient hypothesis? If you'll permit me an overly simplistic definition, the hypothesis is this: we work harder to achieve a goal when the goal is in sight. This is how Olympic runners who have been sprinting an entire race reach down and find an even faster gear the final 100 meters before the finish line. The hypothesis applies to things such as customer reward programs and even corporate bonuses.

Read 1 John 3:1-3. Here John helps us grasp the wonder of our transformation. When we come to saving faith in Jesus, our status changes. We go from sinner to saint, just like that. But that is not the only transformation. When we experience salvation, we go from an orphan to a member of God's family. Paul deals with this as well, but John is essentially saying here that through His great love, God welcomes us into His family as children, with all the rights of children. We share in the inheritance of our Father. This is a profound change, but John goes on to tell us just how far-reaching this change is.

Don't miss vs. 2. John says here that our transformation is so complete, that it's not just for today, but for forever. When John says that "what we will be has not yet appeared," he is referring to our glorification. This is the hope of our transformation that there is a day coming when God will gather all of His children to Him for eternity. In the eternity that we will share with God, we will be perfected. Our bodies will be free from the effects of sin: death, disease, decay, and so on. Our souls will be unmarred by sin's stain. We will be forever united with God in perfection. This is our hope. This is the future of our transformation.

It is easy to focus all of our discipleship efforts on the present, and for a good reason. It's where we are! We live in this physical, temporal world. We strive to be the best we can be. Much of this book will challenge you to give your all at being a disciple, husband, son, father, employee, and so on. It's God's call on us and the expectation of all Christians. Being a disciple means never letting up in our pursuit of God and in our pursuit of what God has given us influence over. But we must consider that this life is not the end goal. It's not our forever home.

Far from being an abstract concept, it's one that should give us strength and encouragement each day. It certainly did for the early Christians. The goal of eternal life in the presence of God motivated them to do their work here on earth. What if we lived the same way? My hunch is that it would radically change the culture around us. What's keeping you from living that way?

# DISCIPLE-SHAPING QUESTIONS

1. Do you ever stop and think about what it will be like to be with God forever? To be free from the trials and troubles of this life? How does that make you feel?

2. Describe an aspect of this life we live that can make you weary.

3. How can you adjust the way you think about this aspect and learn to see it in light of the eternity with God that awaits you?

4. The goal-gradient hypothesis is interesting because it shows how athletes empty their tanks when they see the finish line. They don't leave anything on the table. THAT is how we're supposed to live our lives as Christ-followers on this earth. Spend a few minutes envisioning what your marriage would look like if you gave it your all. What would your parenting look like? What would your career look like if you held nothing back? What would your faith look like if you gave everything to God? You can live like this. It's not just possible; it's what God wants from us. And it starts by living life in view of eternity. Let your mind wander a bit. What would it take to adopt this attitude?

# WEEK 2:

# DISCIPLES SURRENDER TO A GOSPEL-CENTERED LIFE

When you think of the word surrender, what comes to mind? Do you picture an army waving a white flag? Do you imagine a football team down four TD's in the 4th quarter? Or maybe it's the feeling you get right before you break down and admit that the home improvement project you're in the middle of was too complicated for you after all. We know what surrender looks like. And in the real world, it's never good. But God's world isn't the real world, and His values aren't the world's values.

One of the traits of a disciple is the realization that discipleship isn't about what God can do for you. Being an authentic disciple of Christ is ultimately about surrender. It's about giving up the control of your life and letting God lead, as He alone is uniquely suited to lead. In place of a life where you're at the center, you're called to live a life where Christ is at the center, where the Gospel is at the center.

The Gospel translates as the "good news." The good news about Jesus. The good news that we who were once enemies of God have become friends. We who were dead have become alive. The Gospel message is about grace, love, and victory. As a man seeking to be a faithful follower of Christ, the Gospel message should be central in your life. Every aspect of who you are should be dripping with the Gospel, which doesn't happen without surrender.

*This week, Rich Wingo will help you understand what it means that disciples must surrender to a Gospel-centered life.*

# WEEK 2 DAY 1

SCRIPTURE PASSAGE: EZEKIEL 3:16-19

When I played football for the University of Alabama, Coach Paul "Bear" Bryant would walk through the quiet, nervous locker room before each of our games. Periodically he would rest his hand on a player's shoulder and quietly say, "be a difference-maker today." He would only say it a few times throughout the year. As a freshman, I always wondered what he meant by being a difference-maker. Then, in a team meeting, I found out what Coach Bryant meant. I remember him explaining that a difference-maker is someone who plays each play as if the game depends upon him: his winning tackle, his winning block, his winning catch, or run, and so on. He puts the game on his back. His mindset is simply, "it's on me." If you have 11 players on the field with that single mindset every play, your team is tough to beat.

A disciple of Jesus Christ is the poster child for a difference-maker. Read Ezekiel 3:16-19. In Ezekiel 3, God tells Ezekiel that he is to warn those God told him to warn and that if he doesn't, God will hold Ezekiel accountable. For Ezekiel to fulfill his mission, he had to be ALL IN. He had to be fully surrendered to the task God put before him. The same is true for us.

For those of you who are blessed to be husbands and dads, we are called to be difference-makers. And we can't be difference-makers unless we are fully surrendered to our calling. That's why surrender is such a vital aspect of discipleship. Our family's future depends on us. Like it or not, we are the watchman of our family. Nowhere in the Bible can I find such a thing as a godly passive man. It takes hard work and effort to be a man of God! Heads up, men; for some of you, it's time to get off the couch, engage your wife and children, turn off the TV, and invest in your family.

Men, are you praying with your wife daily? Do you have a daily Bible study alone or together? Are you and your family committed to attend Church regularly? If not, can I say in love that you're failing miserably? Your family deserves your best, and your best is not you; it's Christ in and through you.

Imagine Jesus Christ in your presence, putting His hand on your shoulder and saying, "Be a difference-maker today." Have you fully surrendered to being a disciple who makes a difference for God's sake?

# DISCIPLE-SHAPING QUESTIONS

1. Describe your level of surrender to the Gospel.

2. What in your life are you holding back from God?

3. What will it take for you to truly surrender your life to Jesus, EVERY aspect of it?

4. Pray today that you would begin to see yourself as a difference-maker. Ask God to give you the strength to become the man He intends you to be.

# WEEK 2 DAY 2

SCRIPTURE PASSAGE: HEBREWS 12:12-17

Some time ago, I found myself tagging along with my friend Rick Burgess. We were headed to speak at a men's conference in Mobile, AL. That Friday night, Rick brought a convicting message from Mathew 7:13-14. Rick asked men if they were going to travel the narrow, difficult road of following Christ or the wide, easy road that leads to destruction. Rick gave an invitation, and men flooded the altar. I found myself sharing the Gospel to one man after another, inviting them to Christ. It was AWESOME. But what I will never forget was a man on his face at the foot of the altar. He was not weeping; he was wailing, calling out to Jesus. As I kneeled to console him, I realized the sound I was hearing was the sound of regret. It is a sound I will never forget and one I hope I never hear again.

Read Hebrews 12:12-17. Recall that Jacob and Esau were the twins born to Isaac and Rebecca. Esau was a man's man. The Bible tells us he was a big, strong man who loved to hunt and be outside. Esau believed in God. After all, his grandpa was Abraham, and his dad was Isaac. Not a bad legacy. But remember, Esau disgraced himself when he sold his father's blessing to Jacob for a bowl of stew. This may not seem like a big deal to us, but it was back then.

Hebrews 12:17 takes us to the end of Esau's life, where we see that he tried in vain to undue the mistake of his past. But he was too late. The opportunity had passed by. Gentleman, as you seek to be a true disciple, don't play games with God. God has no time for men who have one foot in the world and one foot in God's Kingdom. Esau was that guy that said, "I will get right with the big man upstairs one day, but for now, I love my life." Like many men, Esau believed in God but didn't have enough regard for God to take Him seriously. We cannot be like Esau in this way. At the end of his life, we see Esau full of regret. That was what I heard that night in Mobile.

No real disciple loves the things of this world over God. Authentic followers of Christ surrender their heart's to God and His ways. If you need to repent of a divided heart, now is the time. The man I saw broken that night in Mobile? He experienced genuine repentance, and God, in His grace, granted him forgiveness through His Son Jesus Christ. Praise God it was not too late to come to the throne of Christ. Where are you in all of this? Are you living a life like Esau, a life of eventual regret? If so, my prayer is that right now, you surrender to God for genuine repentance and that God would hear your prayer.

# DISCIPLE-SHAPING QUESTIONS

1. Is your heart divided? Are you only giving God some of your heart? Now is the time to repent. If this describes you, repent now. Pray to God and ask forgiveness for your half-hearted pursuit of Him.

2. What is the best way to not have any spiritual regrets?

3. Do you have regrets? Why? Answer in the space below.

4. If you've asked God to forgive you, you are forgiven. Being a disciple of Christ is moving forward in faith, desiring to be used by God. Spend a moment in prayer thanking God that, if you have come to saving faith in Jesus, He sees you as holy because of the work Jesus did on your behalf on the cross. Spend a moment thanking God for His approval. Accept His love for you and recommit to serving Him.

# WEEK 2 DAY 3

SCRIPTURE PASSAGE: JUDGES 6:11-17

A few years ago, my wife Cheri and I were helping my parents move from their home to an assisted living facility when mom handed me a stack of unopened letters. These were letters sent to me at my parents' home that had been untouched for 40 years. When we returned home, I put the letters in a drawer and forgot about them. Years later, I ran across them. Curious, I began to flip through the letters when I saw a letter from Coach Bryant dated July 22, 1977. Sitting there on the edge of our couch all these years later, I couldn't help but be excited.

I opened the envelope to find a form letter typed on Alabama Football letterhead telling us when to report for fall camp, the importance of being prepared, and so on. It was special reading Coach Bryant's words, and I remember thinking that I needed to give the letter to the Bryant Museum. That was until I turned to the second page. At the bottom of the page, written in black magic marker, was a handwritten note from Coach Bryant. It said, "It is late, but you can still be the player predicted. Hoping and praying you do." Whoa, wait a minute. What did I just read? Not the player predicted? I couldn't believe it. Forty years later, Coach was still kicking my butt. I couldn't help but wonder if I was a disappointment to him. I mean, I was the starting inside linebacker. I believe we were the #1 or #2 team in the country. For weeks, I remember wishing I had never opened the letter.

Because God loved Israel, He disciplined them for their rebellion against Him. In Judges, we learn that God allowed the Midianites to harass Israel while the Israelites would hide in caves out of fear for their pathetic lives. But that was about to change. Read Judges 6:11-17. Here God called on the least likely man to lead His people against the Midianites. His name was Gideon. In Judges 6:11, we find Gideon threshing wheat in a winepress because he was so scared of the Midianites. Gideon protests to God, telling Him that He had made a terrible mistake choosing him. But God knows best. God saw what Gideon could be, not what he was. God was calling the champion out in Gideon. Champions act differently, speak differently, and live differently. Champions inspire. Gideon would become a champion. But first, he had to believe he could be.

I am so thankful all these years later that Coach Bryant cared enough to discipline and challenge me. You see, he saw something in me I never saw in myself. He saw what I could be, not what I was. He wanted my best. Do you have any idea of the ability you have in Christ to bless those around you? God saw the potential in Gideon. You and I see our weaknesses and limitations, but God sees our potential. God calls out the champion in you. How are you going to respond?

# DISCIPLE-SHAPING QUESTIONS

1. Part of surrendering to the Gospel is believing that God honors your desire to bring your best to Him. How do you see God taking what you would see as a weakness and making it a strength?

2. When God chose to use Gideon, God found him hiding in fear. What fears do you have that you need to surrender to God?

3. Do you want to see God use you in powerful ways? Have you told Him so? Have you verbalized to God that you want your life to count for something more than it is? If not, do so now. Then, expect God to honor your desire. Get ready!

# WEEK 2 DAY 4

SCRIPTURE PASSAGE: JOSHUA 1:16-18

As a skinny freshmen linebacker, I will never forget hearing coach Bryant say after practice, "Gentlemen, after today, you'll be able to write home to your mommas that you ran fifty 50-yard sprints." All I could think about after three weeks of gut-wrenching two-a-day practices under the smoking hot Alabama sun was that I am not going to make it.

Shuffling like a zombie with my teammates to the 50-yard line, ready to quit, an (eventual) All- American upperclassmen came up to me, grabbed my shoulder pads, and said, "Stay with me. Do what I do. We got this." The whistle blew, and we began to run. My shoes had so much sweat in them that it sounded like I was running in water. I followed the upperclassman, focusing on one sprint at a time, and by God's grace, I somehow managed to live to tell this story. I would never have made it had it not been for my teammate coming alongside me that day. I was ready to give up something I truly loved.

Read Joshua 1:16-18. The people of Israel have just buried Moses, their leader. God has chosen Joshua to lead them into the Promised Land after 40 years of wandering. Joshua had huge shoes to fill, and it seems here like he is not sure he has what it takes. But then, in vs. 16, the people of Israel say to Joshua that they will follow him just as they followed Moses. Did you get that? God sent His people to tell Joshua that they had his back, but on one condition: Joshua had to lead faithfully.

Do you have a brother that loves you enough that will come alongside you in impossible times in your life, times when you're ready to quit? Satan will do everything possible to prevent you from having this type of relationship, but I challenge you to begin to pray for this. Men, your wife, your children, maybe even your grandchildren are standing in front of you right now saying, "we will follow you, on one condition: you must be in the will of God." We need men in our lives to encourage and support us.

As a disciple of Jesus, who do you see that's struggling? Who is ready to give up like I was that day years ago on the practice field? When you spot these men, are you willing to come alongside and be that guy that says, "we got this, follow me"? It's our job as men of God to finish life strong, not holding anything back, to live our life leaning into the finishing line, to finish completely empty, exhausted for the Kingdom of God.

# DISCIPLE-SHAPING QUESTIONS

1. Surrendering to the Gospel means living a life where we leave it all on the line for the sake of the Kingdom. Does this describe your faith life?

2. As you seek to be a more faithful disciple of Jesus, think of a man in your life who needs encouragement. How can you come alongside him today and be that voice of strength?

3. Are you tired spiritually? God has the means to fill you back up. But you have to admit it and turn to Him. If you're worn out, let God know. Ask Him to recharge your batteries. And maybe to send someone to you to help as a fellow servant in pursuit of godliness.

# WEEK 2 DAY 5

SCRIPTURE PASSAGE: ROMANS 7:14-8:2

They had predicted a few snow flurries that winter morning in 2015, but no accumulation. At least that's what the weatherman said as I drove out of the driveway for my daily 60-mile commute to work. Living in the deep south, snow is not our friend, and by 11 am that morning, as the snow came down in blankets, I headed home. Two hours later, and only three blocks from where I started, I knew I was in for a long day. I watched as car after car tried to make it up a minor incline, only to fail and slide back down. The snow blocked every interstate, side road, and neighborhood road. Nine hours later, I found myself-pulling into the same driveway I so confidently left from earlier that morning, exhausted.

Here's my fear as you read this book on what it means to be a disciple: your true desire is to be a man of God, but you continue to face one spiritual roadblock after another in your life. You have a desire to study God's Word, but you are experiencing minimal growth in Christ. You have a desire to serve others, but you struggle with following through. And as a result, you're making little impact. If this describes you, you are not alone.

Read Romans 7:14-8:2. Here, Paul tells us that he struggles with the same tension between what he wants to do and what he does. Paul is telling us that the sole issue for our separation from our Lord and Savior is the sin in our lives. We sin because we choose to sin. We choose to sin because we love our sin. It's our nature to sin. How do we stop feeding sin and begin to starve the desire to do what is evil? The answer is in Romans 8:1-2.

If you have come to saving faith in Jesus, you belong to God. And when you belong to God, the power of the Spirit frees you from the power of sin. When you and I feel overwhelmed by sin's appeal, let us claim the freedom Christ gave us through the Holy Spirit. While we will never be perfect, allowing the Spirit to take control of our lives removes the roadblocks one by one.

Imagine a full clear glass of milk in your hand. Now imagine pouring chocolate syrup into the milk. Can you see the chocolate settling to the bottom of the glass? The chocolate is inside the glass, but the milk is still mostly white. Now take a spoon and begin to stir. The milk slowly begins to transform. Many of us believe in Jesus Christ and have accepted Him as our Savior. We have His Spirit in our lives. But only when we surrender to the Spirit and allow Him to stir up our lives will we see a radical transformation. Only then will we begin to experience the power of victory over sin.

# DISCIPLE-SHAPING QUESTIONS

1. What desires do you have when it comes to your faith? What do you wish were true about you? Write some of these down.

2. Now, ask yourself, what is keeping these from being true? What stands in the way of each of the things you listed? Again, write these down.

3. Spend some time in prayer today, surrendering these roadblocks to God. Ask Him to remove them, and believe that He will. Commit to a greater level of surrender than the one you currently offer God. EXPECT God to move and for Him to begin to make you the person you want to be.

# WEEK 3:

# DISCIPLES HUNGER TO KNOW GOD

Do you strive to live a godly life? Or just a good life? There's a difference.

If we aren't careful, we can slip into a God-less Christianity. How is that possible? It's more common than you might think. It happens when we find our actions motivated by working to be "moral" instead of seeking to imitate Christ. Now do you get it?

Seeking to be good and not godly is a kind of legalism. And it happens when we become disconnected from God and His Word. When men stop trying to know God through reading the Bible and communicating with Him through prayer, they become people who no longer live like God. This is not an option for men seeking to be disciples.

Authentic disciples have a hunger to know God. To have His heart. To see the world through His eyes. To serve as His hands. That's what Paul meant in Ephesians 5 when he called us to be God-imitators! But the tough reality is that we can't imitate God if we don't know what He looks like.

God didn't just give us Scripture as the "handbook for life," or as "a love letter," or any of the other well-meaning but misguided ways of describing His Word. The Bible is so much more. God gave us His Word as the primary means of revealing Himself to us. Through meeting God in His Word, we come as close to a face-to-face encounter as possible this side of Heaven. Through prayer, we communicate with God in the intimate conversation of relationship. In these disciplines, we can know God, truly know our Creator!

*Over the next five days, Chad Poe will show you that a hunger for knowing God is a vital trait in the lives of His disciples.*

# WEEK 3 DAY 1

SCRIPTURE PASSAGE: PSALM 63:1

Do you have an example of wanting something so badly it affected you physically? I had the opportunity to visit Israel. For numerous reasons, it changed my life. The trip lasted seven days, and it rained seventy-six percent of the time. There is a multitude of pictures of me walking around, dripping wet. Between tour stops, we would eat. When I say eat, I mean, EAT. For us, every meal had five courses. I ate hummus, pita, and falafels. There were pastries and cheeses and kosher meats. The only thing that got me home was my family and bacon. While I was in Israel, I was soaking wet, full of delicious food, and thirsting for nothing.

My condition was the exact opposite of David's in Psalm 63. Read all of the psalm but focus on vs. 1. Jerusalem is not known for rain. Our tour guide pointed out that the phrase, "Rain, rain, go away!" is a phrase they would never use. The idea of God providing water as a means of blessing runs through the scriptures. Yet here, David tells us he is dry. He is hungry. He is thirsty. In this verse, David is using active language to convey a quaking body in desperate need. He tells us that he is persistently pursuing the Lord, and anything short of Him will not satisfy.

When we keep reading this psalm, we see this persistent pursuit of God is met with God's faithfulness. I beheld your power and glory. You gave me fat and rich foods-that is the good stuff. I cling to you. David is longing for the Lord in this dry season even though he knows God is there and that God is good. He knows that the more he seeks God, the more of God he will find. David realizes the goodness God gives is worth his persistence. He knows God's faithfulness is inexplicably greater than his own failures. He knows God and knows that, in this life, there will always be more of God to know.

How about you? If family and friends were to tell people about you, would a phrase like, "That guy is fighting to know God!" ever come out of their mouths? God wants us to hunger after Him because God knows He satisfies. He knows that a hunger and thirst for righteousness will fill us.

# DISCIPLE-SHAPING QUESTIONS

1. What keeps you from seeking after God? What steps do you take to eliminate those distractions?

2. What is an example of a time in your life where you craved God?

3. Can you identify two or three things that are different about then than right now?

4. There may be no more important spiritual practices than connecting with God through Bible reading and prayer. If you have seen these habits slip in your life, pray to God today and ask Him to give you the strength and encouragement to reestablish these traits. If these are habits that are present in your life, pray that God would give you an even deeper desire for knowing Him.

# WEEK 3 DAY 2

I am a sports fan. I have favorite teams, favorite athletes, favorite fantasy football strategies, and favorite gameday snacks. I'm serious. I love sports, and I always have. Basketball and football are my favorites. I prefer lightning-fast offenses that move the ball down the field. I love breakaway basketball that doesn't chew up the shot clock in isolation. I love to see a ferocious attack of the goal.

Read Philippians 3:8-11. Here Paul tells us that his entire life was about a ferocious pursuit of one goal: to be approved by God for his right behavior. He tells us he was the best Pharisee who found pleasure in persecuting the church. He was also the best Jewish person. His behavior was blameless. Paul pursued his goal at a breakneck pace. And he was winning. Until, on the road to Damascus, he realized he was losing. Badly.

In Acts 9, Jesus interrupts Paul as he fast-breaks toward his goal of persecuting the church. In not so many words, Jesus tells Paul that, in all of his Torah knowing, Christian persecuting, and Pharisee hat-wearing, he is actually missing the goal. Not only is he missing the goal, but he is also running in the wrong direction. Paul's pursuit of righteousness missed Jesus. If you miss Jesus, you miss righteousness altogether.

What is the result of Paul's encounter with Jesus? Life change. Paul tells us in Philippians that anything that wasn't aimed at him knowing God better was rubbish. Paul had begun to apply all of his vigor and intellect into knowing Jesus. The wrong goal of Acts 9 (righteousness through the law) had been replaced by righteousness through faith in the death and resurrection of Jesus. Paul's zeal did not change. The object of his zeal did.

Men, in our world where Christian culture clouds and confuses, there is a good chance that lots of well-meaning men are missing Jesus. How many of us grew up speaking of Jesus but having no idea what we were talking about? How many of us identify ourselves as Christians but are not pressing on toward the goal of the upward call of God in Christ Jesus (Philippians 3:14)? If you want to live your life as a disciple, it's time to get real about knowing Him.

# DISCIPLE-SHAPING QUESTIONS

1. If you were to list out the great achievements of your life, what would that list look like?

2. What if you went back to this list and circled any achievement that, though important, was a distraction to knowing Jesus? What would your list look like?

3. The truth for most men is that our pursuit of Jesus is secondary to our pursuit of financial security and accomplishment. While there is certainly nothing wrong with working hard, providing for your family, and setting goals, none of these things are supposed to compete with your all-out devotion to Jesus. Why do you think we as men struggle with this?

4. Do you need to re-prioritize your life? Has your pursuit of Jesus taken a back seat to your pursuit of worldly things? If so, pray that God would convict you of this and give you the strength you need to reorder your life. The stakes are too high to allow anything to come between you and your pursuit of Jesus.

# WEEK 3 DAY 3

SCRIPTURE PASSAGE: PSALM 1:1-2

When I think about high school, I think of the cafeteria. I vividly remember where I would sit each day while I ate my rectangular pizza and drank my sweet tea. My table was made up of me, my best friend Kevin, his high school girlfriend (I didn't have one) who was a year behind us, and a revolving door of kids in her class. At the table next to us, there was Skip, Matthew, and Dale, each aspiring high school politicians who were as likable as anyone could be. To their left were the cheerleaders and the popular girls. Next to them were the athletes and guys with good hair (it was the early 90s, which meant they had bangs that restricted their vision). While there was the occasional interaction between tables, everyone kept to their lunch table (and really any time where teachers did not assign seats). We were known by the company we kept, and our worldview, for better or worse, was shaped accordingly.

Read Psalm 1:1-2. When we meet David in the first psalm, he writes about how our worldview could be affected by our company. "Blessed" is the Hebrew word for "happy." David gives us a progression (or digression) of happiness based on your interactions. A happy man does not move from place to place with those who give bad advice (counsel). Why? Bad advice leads to bad action (sinner). The more we sin, the more we roll our eyes at the fact that sin is sin (scoffer). We are shaped by our consistent experience.

The reverse is also true. We are shaped by the experiences that lead us toward God. David tells us the delight of a happy person comes from God's Word. However, we don't just read it to be informed. Through meditating on it, we are transformed. We do not just read Scripture to have something in our heads; we read it and interact with God through what He has taught us. The happy man does not just free his mind of all thoughts. The happy man knows through filling his mind with God's thoughts that he will be free.

# DISCIPLE-SHAPING QUESTIONS

1. What are you doing in your life to actively avoid the digression this passage shows us of walking with the wicked, standing with sinners, and becoming someone who scoffs at sin?

2. What does daily Bible study look like for you? Describe your daily habits.

3. What does your ability or inability to answer that previous question say about your relationship with God's Word?

4. When a biblical command makes you uncomfortable, how do you respond? What does this say about the condition of your heart and your desire to know God's Word?

# WEEK 3 DAY 4

SCRIPTURE PASSAGE: PHILIPPIANS 4:6-7

I was 25 years old, sitting beside my brother as he lay in a hospital bed. In March of the previous year, he was diagnosed with cancer. In August, our family knew the cancer was terminal. It was now April, and every night, I sat in his hospital room, confused and afraid. In his short life, he had struggled with substance abuse and numerous run-ins with the police. I was mad, sad, and exhausted. I held his hand, which struck me as funny because there is no way he would let me do that if he were healthy.

I kept begging God to help me understand why this was happening. I had lost my mom when I was sixteen. I didn't have an incredibly close relationship with my dad due to his struggles with drugs and alcohol. In my head, it did not have to be this way. My grandmother made sure my brother and I were at church every Sunday. We heard the same stories and had the same teachers. We had the same things swirling around in our minds as to what was good, right, and God-honoring. Yet here I sat, confused.

Read Philippians 4:6-7. By God's grace, people made me memorize parts of the Bible. It was in the sterile quiet of a fourth-floor hospital room where the reality of God's peace transcending all understanding became real to me. The word "transcend" comes from a word tied to exertion. It can mean to outlast or outrun. The most literal definition is to "throw beyond the mark." Philippians is full of verses about athletic exertion. One of the original Olympic games was the discus, and winning in this event came down to a simple measurement. Could you throw the discus further than the other guys? Was the mark your discus made "beyond the mark" of everyone else?

Paul tells us that when we pray, we are training ourselves to interact with the difficulties of life in a fallen world. Through talking to God, expressing gratitude to God, and at times begging God, we will see God's peace outlast our understanding. We will sense it and find comfort in it even though we will not be able to explain why.

That night with my brother, this Scripture hit me in a way it had not before. In a way that is hard to explain, I was reminded that the God who inspired Paul to write these words knew me. On one of my darkest days, the peace of God shined its brightest. It overthrew the mark of my understanding.

# DISCIPLE-SHAPING QUESTIONS

1. Why do you think some people find prayer to be a difficult spiritual habit?

2. Write down a moment where the truth of God's peace amid hardship and confusion became real to you.

3. What is the connection between prayer, Bible reading, and God's comfort?

4. What are ways to remind yourself of the faithfulness of God when the next storm comes up?

# WEEK 3 DAY 5

Like every child ever, my kids love holidays. My crew is always ready to celebrate. It will come as no surprise to you that they enjoy holidays that involve gifts the most. I am glad they do not know what Arbor Day is. With four kids, I would have a forest in my front yard.

They love gifts. They love to give them. They love to get them. They try to keep you posted on their wish lists. Thankfully, we have a rule that says, "If you tell us what you want, you probably won't get it." Though the rule is really to teach our kids that you don't always get what you want, a secondary effect is that it cuts down gift chatter. As much as every parent wants to have lengthy, meaningful conversations with their children about puppies, Nintendo Switches, and snake tongs (true story), my ears can only handle so much.

Read Colossians 4:2. In Colossians, Paul shows us God wants to hear from us, He wants to shape what He hears, and that He never is never exhausted with us. Isaiah 40 tells us God does not grow weary in any of the ways human beings do. This includes His ability to listen without growing tired. God not only wants to give His children gifts; His choosing to hear from us is a gift. On top of that, His Word shows us the best ways to interact with Him.

Praying watchfully is really about paying attention to a couple of things. First, we are to be aware of the needs around us and consider others' needs as we interact with God. In my own life, focused prayer concerning people other than myself is an afterthought. Paul is encouraging us to talk to God about the situations we see taking place every day. Secondly, we are to be attentive to thank God for the things we see Him do. It is incredibly easy to miss God's blessing because I am more concerned about my next pressing need.

In our Philippians passage from yesterday, Paul uses another word to talk about prayer I don't want us to overlook. He tells us to pray "with supplication." This word means to "humbly beg and plead." This is not something comfortable for most men. We pick ourselves up by our bootstraps and "get the job done." Whenever Paul talks about prayer, he is showing us how helpless we are. We need God to move. We should want God to move. We have no other options if God does not move.

# DISCIPLE-SHAPING QUESTIONS

Open your Bible to the Lord's Prayer. Spend some time walking through it personally.

1. "Our Father in Heaven . . . " How do you understand God as your Father through Jesus?

2. "Hallowed be your name . . . " Write down words that come to mind when you think about God.

3. "Your Kingdom come, your will be done . . . " In what ways are you asking for God's Kingdom to come and acting in line with that?

4. "Give us this day our daily bread . . . " Thank God for how He has provided for you.

5. "Forgive us our debts as we forgive our debtors . . . " Thank God for His forgiveness. Think through who you need to forgive.

6. "Lead us not into temptation but deliver us from evil . . ." Proactively consider the upcoming week so you can combat sin that is around the corner.

# WEEK 4:

# DISCIPLES DESIRE TO WORSHIP GOD

How would you define worship? It's one of those "we know it when we see it" situations, isn't it? When it comes to worship, it's not that we don't know how to define it. It's that our definitions are often too narrow. But worship is an essential trait of a disciple. If we are to be men who are faithful followers of Christ, we have to know what we mean when we talk about worshipping God.

A desire to worship God goes way beyond what men do in church on Sunday mornings. For the man seeking to be a disciple of God, worship should be understood as simply this: a right response to who God is. Your life intersects with God in many different ways. You encounter Him in His Word. You can think about Him on your way to work or to the gym. You experience or are aware of blessings from God as you interact with friends and family. You see God in His creation, and so on. When you encounter God in these ways, when you behold Him, so to speak, your response is worship.

If worship is your response to God when you encounter Him, and you encounter God all around you every day, then we can quickly see that worship must go beyond the sanctuary on Sunday mornings. You can and should worship God in the car, alone, with your thoughts or words. But you can also worship God through the manner in which you conduct yourself with your family. You can worship God through corporate praise with your church community. But you can also worship God with friends over coffee or in how you treat your co-workers. A lifestyle of worship is the way an authentic disciple shows God his gratitude. Worship is simply giving back to God what is rightfully His.

*This week, Eric Ballard will walk you through an in-depth look at what it means to have the desire to worship God.*

# WEEK 4 DAY 1

I have been married for a little over 13 years. When I first saw my wife, I simply had to talk to her. It took a few minutes to gather my courage and check my breath; then I walked over to meet her. It was as if I had no choice in the matter. Once I became aware of her, my heart took over and moved me in her direction. It was the right response.

Read Psalm 136:1-3. A bit repetitive, right? There's a reason for that. The psalmist was growing in his understanding of who God is. Because he was a disciple of the LORD, the writer was aware of God's goodness, enduring love, and unrivaled authority. As a response, the author of this song gave thanks with an offering of gratitude he couldn't help but say over and over again. It was an act of worship.

Worship is our response to who God is. We don't come into this world as disciples of God. The opposite is true. We are sinful from birth (Psalm 51:5) and at odds with who God is from our beginning. But once we become aware of our Creator, we respond with worship. Similar to how I was drawn to my wife once I knew of her, as we begin to recognize the God of the universe and His desire to know us, His love will initiate a heart-reaction within us that we can't control. Gratitude, surrender, thanks, praise, submission, honor, obedience—all of these are reactions of worship because they are all ways we can respond to who God is and His presence in our lives.

In his book, The Journey of Desire, John Eldredge wrote, "Worship is the act of the abandoned heart adoring its God." The way you choose to worship may look different than mine or other guys you know, and that is okay. Because we are all created uniquely, we will naturally have different reactions and responses to God. The important thing is that when we choose to follow Jesus as a disciple, our lives become a response of worship to who God is. This outpouring of our hearts is worship, in all its forms.

# DISCIPLE-SHAPING QUESTIONS

1. What are some significant ways you have responded to the work of God in your life? How do you see these actions as a means of worship?

2. How do you most often participate in worshiping the Lord? Why this method?

3. The more aware we are of God, the more opportunities we will have to respond in worship. What could you do to become more aware of God's presence around you?

4. Do something different. Try an act of worship you haven't before. Try writing a prayer/poem/song of praise to God. Or the next time you are at your church worship service, you could sing louder and prouder, raise your hands, or sit down and pray while the songs of praise from others swim around you. Whatever you do, stretch your comfort zone of worship. It just may help you connect to God in a new way.

# WEEK 4 DAY 2

"Are you crying? ARE YOU CRYING? There's no crying. There's no crying in baseball!" Tell me you know this quote. In case you are unfamiliar, it's from the movie *A League of Their Own*. In this gem, Tom Hanks plays the manager of an all-girls baseball team. In between innings of one particular game, he berates one of his players for a mistake she made. Afterward, she immediately breaks down and starts crying. Hanks' character can't believe it. In his opinion, it was universally understood that crying was an emotion that simply wasn't allowed on the ballfield.

Many men live their lives with similar unwritten rules as baseball. There's this not-so-secret stereotypical idea floating around that to be manly, a code of guidelines must be followed. For starters, there's no crying. Regardless of the circumstances, men should never express certain emotions. Giving in to our feelings is seen as a sign of weakness. It's almost as if this perception of a stoic man has been passed down from father to son in unspoken terms for generations. If we're honest, simply being around a man who is crying or openly expressing his feelings can make us feel at least a little uncomfortable. Why is that?

The great men of the Bible didn't seem to live by this Bro Code. David is arguably one of the greatest warriors the world has ever known. Taking down a literal giant with a slingshot and a rock builds quite the reputation (1 Sam. 17:48-49). But as the writer of many psalms, David was also a sensitive poet. Instead of the electric guitar or drums, David played the harp—not the manliest of instruments (1 Sam. 16:18). He also had no reservations about baring his heart to his friend, Jonathan (1 Sam. 20). Abraham expressed feelings of vulnerability to his wife (Gen. 12:11-13). Moses had feelings of inadequacy (Exod. 3:11) and openly admitted his fear (Heb. 12:21).

Jesus was perfect, the perfect man. And His flawless love expressed itself in a broad spectrum of emotions. Jesus got angry and sad (Mark 3:5). He wept (John 11:35). He got tired (John 4:6). He felt empathy and compassion for others (Luke 7:13). Jesus was a happy guy (Luke 10:21). And He was also well acquainted with the feelings associated with humility (John 13:3-5; Phil. 2:8).

Read Psalm 103:1-2. The phrase "all my inmost being" implies that we should be fully emotionally engaged in our worship of God. No holding back. A disciple of Jesus follows His great example, and Jesus lived out a life of worship towards His Heavenly Father expressed through all His emotions. If we think a man shouldn't express his feelings, maybe it's because we have the wrong concept of manhood.

# DISCIPLE-SHAPING QUESTIONS

1. Many men have two emotions: angry and not angry. What feelings do you have the most challenging time trying to express? Why do you think that is? Do you see this as a weakness or strength? Explain your answer.

2. How does expressing your emotions (or lack thereof) affect your family? What do you think they are learning about you from what you don't say?

3. Our faith shouldn't be based on emotions, but it should include emotions. How do you think your feelings or emotions could help enhance your times of worship with the Lord? What emotions arise in you when you read about the promises God has made to you in His Word?

4. If you could hear your dad say one thing to you, what would it be? Do your best to say those words to your family. Don't hold back the words they need to hear from you.

# WEEK 4 DAY 3

SCRIPTURE PASSAGE: PSALM 43:3-4

I hate dancing. It's stupid. If you feel differently, it's probably because you are good at it or have at least a sliver of rhythm. I don't. And it shows every single time I find myself on a dance floor. All my "moves" are mechanical and forced. There's no excitement or joy while I sway about with zero coordination. And that fact is apparent to everyone involved.

Next time you go to church, take a quick survey of the men in your gathering as they rise to their feet to participate in the worship service. Look at their facial expressions. Check out their body language. Examine your own as well. Chances are, they have the same approach to worship as I do to dance: "Well, if I have to, I'll force my way through this thing."

Worship was never meant to be something we simply tried to grin-and-bear our way through. Worship is not the time to merely go through the motions. Read Psalm 43:3-4. The writer of this song views worshiping at the altar of God with great joy. It is a cause for celebration. When we turn worship into nothing more than mumbling words off a screen or out of a hymnal, we've missed the incredible opportunity we have. Worship as a response to God can stir wonder in us as nothing else can.

There was a time in Israel's history when the ark of the Lord, a symbol of God's presence on earth, was stolen away from His people. While David was king, he restored the ark to Jerusalem. As the ark entered the city gates, David, overcome with joy, danced before the Lord with all his might (2 Sam. 6:14). There's a guy who understood worship! Experiencing the presence of the Lord moved David to celebrate.

Part of the reason I hate dancing is that I know I look ridiculous doing it. If I could ever let go of that self-conciseness, I just might enjoy cutting a rug. Maybe we act constrained when it comes to worship because we are self-conscious about how we may look. We should take a note from David. He didn't care how he looked in worship. He even told his wife, who did not appreciate the king's dance moves, he was willing to look utterly undignified if it was in worship of the King of Kings (2 Sam. 21-22).

Disciples of Jesus find joy in His presence. As we learn to let go of ourselves to embrace Him in worship, celebration will follow. It may not move us to dance, but it will *move* us.

# DISCIPLE-SHAPING QUESTIONS

1. We need to understand that worshiping God isn't about us. How others respond to us should not influence how we respond to God. How can letting go of self-conscious thoughts or feelings free us up for a more genuine worship experience?

2. What brings you the greatest joy in your relationship with Jesus? How do you express that to Him?

3. Read Philippians 4:11-13. In this passage, Paul wrote about being content whether he had plenty or in need. How can contentment in God's blessings in your life bring about joy?

# WEEK 4 DAY 4

SCRIPTURE PASSAGE: ROMANS 12:1-2

Years ago, when my oldest daughter was four, she had a real problem staying seated for meals at the table. She would stand up, walk around, dance, perform the occasional cartwheel, anything but sit. We addressed this in many long, repetitive talks. Finally, she sat through a whole meal. I couldn't have been prouder. Not long after her victorious sit-down, we went out to eat at her favorite restaurant. Once again, she was standing and moving about while she ate. I asked her what she was doing and why wasn't she sitting like before. Her response was, "I thought that was just supposed to be for our house."

When it comes to worship, many of us have the same idea about it as my daughter did with sitting at the table; it's just supposed to be for God's house. But that is a limited view on worship. Honoring God through worship stretches far beyond the sanctuary walls of our church. Remember that worship is simply our response to God and His presence in our lives. Because we can encounter God everywhere, we can respond to Him (worship) everywhere. And we should.

Read Romans 12:1-2. In this passage, Paul informs us that we are to become "living sacrifices" as our offering of worship to the Lord. This means more than singing praise songs and hymns on a Sunday morning. As we grow in our discipleship of Jesus, our worship will grow to become part of our daily living (living sacrifices).

If it is for the Lord, practically everything can be an act of worship. In a couple of his other letters, Paul stressed this point of endless possibilities to worship in our daily living in whatever we do (Col. 3:17). This includes how we speak, treat other people, lead our families, encourage friends or neighbors, and how we conduct ourselves at work (Col. 3:23). To further this idea, Paul went so far as to say that we can even do mundane functions like eating and drinking for God's glory (1 Cor. 10:31).

As a disciple of Jesus, we will begin to view worship as a lifestyle lived out in obedience to God. Jesus told His followers, "If you love me, you will keep my commandments" (John 14:15). Disciples display their love and worship for Jesus in everything they do, both inside and outside the church.

# DISCIPLE-SHAPING QUESTIONS

1. In what ways can you worship God at home with your family? At the gym? Out to eat with friends? On vacation? Alone in the car on your commute to work?

2. If you were to take a quick look through the Bible, you would notice many significant encounters people had with God happened outside. How does God's creation speak to you of His glory? In what ways can nature be considered God's most splendid cathedral?

3. A large portion of our waking hours is spent at work. How can you bring worship into the workplace? If you lived in complete obedience to God at your job, what difference do you think it would make in your life? What about in the lives of your co-workers?

4. Reread Romans 12:1-2. Paul states being transformed will help us recognize what God's will is. How have you been able to recognize God's will in your life? What could you do that might help you identify God's voice more clearly?

5. Just because we know God's will, doesn't mean we follow it. Think about a time you knew you were living outside of God's desire for your life. What were some of the consequences you experienced? What brought you back to the LORD's guidance?

# WEEK 4 DAY 5

SCRIPTURE PASSAGE: COLOSSIANS 3:14-17

You can't see me, but I'm huge! A true goliath of pure muscle. (Don't google me, just take my word for it). One day while I was warming up in the gym, the guy next to me was lifting an insane amount of weight. He loaded his bar up so heavy that I stopped what I was doing to watch. He groaned, grunted, and his face turned weird shades of purple as he strained to raise the bar. I clapped a little at his impressive feat. Then he went for a second rep. This time the bar didn't move. He was trapped under it. I ran over, and we quickly lifted the weight off of him together. This guy was strong, crazy strong, but even he had his limits. What was too heavy for him to handle on his own, we could easily lift together.

Read Colossians 3:14-17. Why do men try to do everything on their own? What is it about us that pushes us into isolation? It's not a healthy lifestyle. From the very beginning, God said, "It is not good that the man should be alone" (Gen. 2:18). If we choose to be a disciple of Jesus all on our own, we may be able to carry the load for a while, but eventually, like the guy in the gym, the weight of it will become too much, and we're going to get stuck. We need someone, a group even, who can help us shoulder the charge.

On a couple of occasions, Jesus sent out His disciples ahead of Him into nearby areas. They were to prepare the towns for Christ's upcoming arrival. When Jesus sent them out, He sent them in pairs. He did this because disciples are stronger together than they are alone (Eccles. 4:9-10).

When we worship God as disciples, it will not only draw us closer to Him, but it will also tug us toward other believers. Worshiping with other Christians stirs us up to love one another and encourages us to keep moving forward in the faith. It is a practice that must not go neglected (Heb. 10:24-25).

There are moments for one-on-one time with God, but there are also times for corporate worship. Both are necessary, and both will make us stronger disciples.

# DISCIPLE-SHAPING QUESTIONS

1. Have you ever had a hard time asking for help? Ever try to do a two-person job by yourself? Of course you have; you're a dude. Spend a few minutes in prayer asking God why this is. Dig in and allow God to show you the roots of these behaviors.

2. Part of what made the original 12 disciples so effective in their mission was that they had each other for accountability and to lean on when things got tough. Who do you have in your life that pushes you closer to God? Who holds you accountable? How do they do this for you?

3. What role do you play in the corporate worship at your church? How engaged are you during the service? What feels different about worshiping with other Christians compared to doing it on your own?

4. Find a group of Christian men. It's great to be part of the church as a whole, but there is something special about being surrounded by godly men. Seek out a men's Bible study or ministry group. Start one if you have to, do whatever it takes to find a community of men who are trying to be disciples of Jesus in the same way you are. If you already have this band of brothers in your life, invite a new guy in.

# DISCIPLES

# PURSUE

# PERSONAL

# HOLINESS

Many Christians have a complicated relationship with holiness. This isn't a recent development. It's a sticking point that reaches back to the roots of God's relationship with us. Here's the crux of the problem: God is holy, and we are not. Yet, holiness is what God expects of us. This is an issue because our inability to be holy serves as a barrier between God and us. But wait! When we come to saving faith in Christ, we're made holy by the work He did on our behalf on the cross. This is good news. But even though God sees us as holy because of what Jesus did for us, we still struggle with sin. See? It's complicated.

As a man who desires to live as an authentic disciple of Christ, we must be committed to pursuing holiness. Yes, if we are in Christ, we are holy in God's eyes. But as Christ-followers, we must contend with our sin, fighting it. Yes, we are covered by God's grace. But Scripture makes it clear that as children of God, our lives are to be lived above reproach. There is no mistaking it. Scripture is clear that we are to pursue holiness in our lives.

This week will challenge you. It will make the biblical case for the pursuit of holiness. And it will call you to pursue it in your daily life. How we think about holiness says a lot about how we approach our faith overall. If you are serious about being the kind of man who is a credit to the Kingdom, this chapter is for you. Are you ready to accept the challenge?

*Turn the page as Rick Burgess helps show you how disciples pursue personal holiness.*

# WEEK 5 DAY 1

SCRIPTURE PASSAGE: EPHESIANS 1:3-4; COLOSSIANS 1:21-22

Let's be honest: when you realized you were going to spend a week talking about holiness, you were uneasy. We tend to live like Scripture's call to holiness doesn't exist, or we see it as an unattainable goal. We go as far as to mock holiness with terms like "holy roller" or "holier than thou." While it is true that people can be sanctimonious at times, we too often use these words against people who challenge our lack of holiness. What if they are simply more committed disciples of Jesus?

Let's lay it out there: God is Holy, and according to Scripture, we are called to be holy. The writer of Hebrews addresses the issue clearly in Hebrews 12:14 by telling us to "strive for peace with everyone, and for the holiness without which no one will see the Lord." Do I have your attention yet? So, without holiness, you and I will not see the Lord? That's what God's Word says.

Men love a challenge. You are likely hoping that I'm about to give you a new list of rules or a new code of conduct that will put you on the path of holiness. That's not going to happen. Instead, read Ephesians 1:3-4. Paul reminds us that it has always been God's desire that we would be holy. How? Through the sacrifice of the Son. Read Colossians 1:21-22. Have you been reconciled to a holy God through your faith in the sacrifice provided by Jesus Christ? If yes, then you are presented as holy and blameless in Christ. That's the key, men. Jesus doesn't make us a better version of ourselves. He makes us like Him! The key here is for you and me to understand that it's Jesus who makes us holy, and as we connect our lives to Jesus, He then produces the holiness in us.

John 15 is very clear when Jesus says, apart from me, you can do nothing. Therefore abide in me, and I will produce the fruit. To abide in Christ means always being connected to Him and always agreeing with Him. We must be found in Christ. We must be made new by Him. Period. Only then will we be holy.

# DISCIPLE-SHAPING QUESTIONS

1. What has been your attitude toward holiness?

2. Why do you think holiness is something that makes us uncomfortable or uneasy?

3. Be honest: is the personal pursuit of holiness a big part of your life as a Christ-follower? Or is it something you don't think a lot about?

4. Spend some time in prayer today asking God to help you begin to tear down any hang-ups you have about pursuing holiness and to birth in you a desire to take holiness seriously.

# WEEK 5 DAY 2

SCRIPTURE PASSAGE: 1 PETER 1:13-16

In this second day of discussing the idea that a disciple of Jesus is a man whose identity is tied to a pursuit of holiness, let's look at the words of Peter, one of the real men of the Bible. We know that Peter is the kind of guy who puts it to us straight and doesn't pull any punches. With this in mind, read 1 Peter 1:13-16.

Is that straight forward enough for you? I can never quite wrap my mind around how easily men can demand excellence in every aspect of their lives, but they are perfectly OK with mediocrity when it comes to their spiritual lives. Peter addresses this mindset head-on when he tells us to prepare our minds for action. Action? Yes! Remember, Peter is addressing disciples of Christ, not the lost. The disciple of Christ has been redeemed by grace through faith, but the battle for holiness is ongoing. We must prepare ourselves to take action to follow Jesus.

Peter then urges us to remember the grace we were given and the new hope we have in Christ. Men, don't be a grace abuser! Paul says in 1 Corinthians 15:10 that he knows the only good in him is due to the grace Jesus showed him. Paul says he desires that this grace will never be in vain! How about you? Has the grace you received from Jesus been in vain? Has God seen any Kingdom return on that grace?

Peter goes on to say that we who have been redeemed are no longer ignorant about our sin. We know better. So if we sin now, we sin as free people who have been set free by God through Christ. We sin of our own free will. Peter delivers the final punch in vs. 16, where he quotes Leviticus 11:44: God expects us to be holy just as He is holy. All of our conduct is to be holy. All of it. How many of us would love to remove the word "all" and replace it with "some"? The only issue is that this isn't an option. Peter says that God is holy. Therefore, if His Spirit now abides in us, there is no conduct that does not include Him. The movie you watched? God watched with you. The song you are singing? You sing it in front of God. The picture on your phone or computer? God knows it's there. All of our conduct is under His authority.

Simply put, you cannot be a faithful disciple of Jesus unless you are committed to pursuing holiness. Why? Because it is what God Himself expects out of you.

# DISCIPLE-SHAPING QUESTIONS

---

1. God's expectation of you is holiness. Complete and utter holiness. How does this make you feel?

2. In Christ, God sees us as holy. But this doesn't let us off the hook. We are expected to pursue holiness in all our conduct. Can you think of some areas where you are disciplined? Areas in which you, along with the Spirit's help, resist temptation and sin? Write these down.

3. Are there areas in which you consistently fail to "take action"? Specific sin habits that trip you up time and again? What is it about these areas that are so difficult to overcome?

4. Would you consider reaching out to a friend today and asking him to help hold you accountable for the sin habit that trips you up? Bringing sin into the light is one of the main ways of defeating it. What is keeping you from doing whatever it takes to break sin's hold on you?

SCRIPTURE PASSAGE: 1 THESSALONIANS 4:1-8

I have always been slightly embarrassed by the fact that I know nothing about automobiles. When I get the call that my wife or one of my children is having car trouble, I am zero help. The best I can do is call a mechanic because I am not one. Not even close. But what if I claimed to be a mechanic?

To prove that I truly was a mechanic, I would have to open the hood and know what I was looking at. I would have to be able to diagnose potential problems based on a description. There would have to be some proof that I was the real deal. If I claimed to be a mechanic but knew nothing about your vehicle, then that claim would be false.

Jesus talks about something very similar in Matthew 7:21-23. Jesus says that not everyone who claims Him to be their Lord is telling the truth. But in vs. 21, He says that people who do the will of the Father will enter the kingdom of heaven. Interesting. So we can't just "claim" to be a disciple of Jesus and it be true. Jesus is clear that those who do the will of His Father are the true disciples.

Read 1 Thessalonians 4:1-8. In verses 1-2, we see that Paul is pleased with the progress of the church. But in vs. 3, he drives home the main point. Re-read that verse. Jesus said that only those who do the will of His Father will inherit the Kingdom of God. Paul says that our sanctification is the will of God. Put those two commands together, and the importance of the pursuit of holiness becomes apparent.

God calls us to be people who are set apart and holy. Those who do not live a holy life are like those who do not know God. Is this sanctification process quick and easy? No, that would be how Jesus described the road to destruction in Matthew 7:13. But for the disciple of Jesus, the desire to be more like Jesus is not a burden. In fact, it is the exact opposite.

I will never forget my wife's revelation when our youngest son died his earthly death. She said that she was talking to God, and she cried out, "but we were so happy," to which God answered, "but I want you to be holy." The disciple of Christ prefers Jesus to any pleasures of his flesh. He seeks peace and joy, not momentary, fleeting moments of happiness. It is a high calling. But it is one that leads to such tremendous fulfillment. Are you willing to know the kind of fulfillment that comes with wholeheartedly pursuing holiness?

# DISCIPLE-SHAPING QUESTIONS

1. Paul gives us a clue in this passage about what we can practically do to pursue holiness. He says that we cannot disregard God's call to holiness. Maybe the first thing you need to do is tell God that you accept His call to holiness. You do not disregard it. You hear it and accept it. If you've never done this, do it now.

2. Ask yourself, "What does it mean that I have heard and accepted God's call for me to pursue holiness"? Reflect on this thought and consider writing down your response.

3. What does it mean to you that if you disregard God's call to take holiness seriously, you're not disregarding man, but God Himself? Is disregarding God something you're willing to be a part of?

4. Consider saying a prayer today expressing to God your deep desire to be more serious about holiness. Don't say it if you don't mean it.

# WEEK 5 DAY 4

SCRIPTURE PASSAGE: 1 JOHN 3:4-8

Jesus tells us quite clearly in John 14:15 that if we love Him, we will obey His commands. Imagine the following scenario: I tell my wife Sherri that I love her every Sunday morning. I sing songs to her, I bring flowers to her, and I spend the morning with her. Then, about lunchtime, I leave her and go my own way for the rest of the week. In the next six and a half days, I spend no time with her. I see other women, devote myself to my hobbies and my work, and pretty much do whatever I choose. Then, on Sunday morning, I get up, find Sherri, tell her I love her again and start the singing and flower giving. Then, about lunchtime, I'm out again.

Would you say this behavior shows that I love my wife? Of course not! And yet, many men act the same way toward Jesus. And these men think that Jesus buys their garbage! Our actions tell us everything we need to know about our love for Christ.

Disciples are devoted to Jesus, not just by their words but in how they live their day-to-day lives. 1 John 3:4-8 is a brutal reminder of this truth. Read these verses. Are they a punch to the gut, or what? Did John just say that those who continue in deliberate, continuous sin have never seen or known Jesus? Wow. Now, John isn't implying that we must be perfect or else we're not Christians. In our fallen world, we will stumble. But the disciple of Christ comes under the Holy Spirit's conviction, repents, and corrects their behavior.

Understand, brother, that if you live a life of deliberate, perpetual sin, it's not because of the lack of the power of Christ to take away that desire and replace it with a desire for Him. It is because you are not abiding in Him. John goes for another punch and reminds us that Jesus makes us fully righteous. If Jesus is fully righteous and God's seed abides in us, then perpetual sin can't rule our lives. Why? The power of God leads us to obedience!

Men, it is evident whether or not you have truly been redeemed and reconciled to a Holy God. Jesus is fully righteous, so He produces righteousness. The Holy Spirit is holy Therefore the seed of God in us produces holiness. Deliberate, perpetual sin does not flow from a person who houses the Spirit of God. It's impossible.

When you look at your life right now, what does the evidence show? Does your commitment to holiness show you to be someone who is redeemed and born again? Or do your actions show that you need to reconsider your relationship with God?

# DISCIPLE-SHAPING QUESTIONS

1. If righteousness is the work of the Spirit through us, we must be people who listen to the Holy Spirit. How is your relationship with the Holy Spirit? Are you used to listening for His leading? How aware are you of His presence in your life?

2. I John 3:6 says this: "No one who abides in [God] keeps on sinning; no one who keeps on sinning has either seen him or known him." In your own words, how is it that we can be saved by faith in Christ and yet still be men who stumble?

3. How do John's words in vs 9 make you feel? John says, "No one born of God makes a practice of sinning." What do your sin habits say about your relationship with Jesus?

4. Continue to do the work of reflection and evaluation of the sin that impacts your life. What work do you need to do? Pray to God to continue to show you places in your life that you've not surrendered to Him.

# WEEK 5 DAY 5

SCRIPTURE PASSAGE: 2 TIMOTHY 2:20-21

Have you ever had to learn something new? One of my sons discovered a passion for lacrosse. I am born and raised in Alabama, and I had no prior experience with the sport. Here's where it got interesting: due to the lack of lacrosse coaches in Alabama, I became the head coach of my son's high school team! I recall once, right in the middle of a game, a player boldly approached me to ask why he wasn't getting to play as much as some of the other players. I reminded him that he had struggled to make plays. I did not play him in key situations because I did not trust him with the responsibility required.

Read 2 Timothy 2:20-21. Do you take the pursuit of holiness seriously? Examine yourself. What are the things in your life that need to be removed in order to be useful to God? Paul says to Timothy that anyone who cleanses himself from what is dishonorable will be a vessel used by God. Yes, we celebrate that we have been saved by grace through faith, but we must understand that this is a faith of action.

I have noticed in my sanctification process that God will convict me of the things that need to be removed from my life. One of the things I have continued to struggle with is gluttony. I have had weight problems for most of my life due to inactivity, overeating, or eating foods of very little nutritional value. God convicted me that I was not just losing weight, eating healthier, and exercising to extend my life; I was doing it to be more effective with my life for the Kingdom of God.

When I was obesely overweight, I lacked credibility trying to teach and lead men. Men could visually see that I lacked self-control. When did I finally take action? When I acknowledged that my gluttony was a sin. I called it sin and realized that I could never truly be holy if I did not take this sin seriously. I took action and continue to this day to fight the battle to eradicate any sin from my life that stands in the way of my sanctification. Does this mean that I am there yet? No. But I no longer justify it in my life. That's the difference. I desire to be a true disciple of Christ. Therefore I take action and pursue holiness.

That is what God desires. That in the moments when it matters, we own our shortcomings and strive to improve. We don't wonder why we're not "in the game." We take stock of our lives, address our weaknesses, and look to get off the sidelines. What behavior do you need to stop justifying? What's keeping you from calling your sin what it is? Whatever it is, you must address it in order to be useful. Until you do, you will never be as useful to God as you could be.

# DISCIPLE-SHAPING QUESTIONS

1. Paul says that if anyone cleanses himself from what is dishonorable, he will be a vessel for honorable use. This is a conditional statement. It could be restated to say, "unless you cleanse yourself from what is dishonorable, you won't be able to be used for honorable purposes." If you've ever wanted to live a more dynamic faith life, have you considered that your lack of meaningful impact might be because of the dishonorable things you hold on to in your life? Think about that for a moment.

2. Truth check time: what are the dishonorable things in your life that need to be cleansed? Do not pass over this question. Take a few minutes and reflect.

3. You wouldn't use a soiled bandage on a fresh wound. You wouldn't wash your car with dirty water. You wouldn't eat spoiled food. And yet, we imagine that we can live sinful lives and still expect God to use us. Do you want to be a useful instrument to God? Then make a plan TODAY to get rid of the dishonorable aspects of your life. Write your plan down if need be. But do whatever it takes to act.

# WEEK 6:

## DISCIPLES

## EMBRACE

## CHRISTIAN

## COMMUNITY

Christian community is more than just hanging out, something that comes naturally to men. Relationships are vital to our lives as men, whether playing with our kids, watching the game with our friends, or eating lunch with co-workers. But Christian community must be deeper than friendship. Christian community is the God-given space in which we're supposed to live out our lives. Over and over again in Scripture, we see God authorizing life done in community. *And this community is to be different than mere friendship; it's supposed to take on the character of God, Himself.*

As men seeking to be disciples, we are called to be devoted to one another, with a faithfulness that mirrors God's. We're called to commit to growing together in our knowledge of God, enjoying each other's fellowship, praying for one another, and meeting each other's needs. But we're also called to the difficult work of community.

If we're honest, this is the part of community that we often leave out. And yet, it may be the very aspect of community that truly separates us from the rest of the world. As Christ-followers, we're called to hold each other accountable, not just for the sin in our lives but for righteousness, as well. We're called to bear each other's burdens, to selflessly put others above ourselves. Christian community is sometimes messy. (OK, Christian community is almost always messy.) But when we fail to embrace it because it's hard, we rob ourselves of the very framework God gave us to make it through this life together.

*This week, Dr. Bryan Gill will lead you to examine what it looks like to embrace Christian community.*

# WEEK 6 DAY 1

SCRIPTURE PASSAGE: MATTHEW 18:20

You've heard it said, "Life is not a sprint; it's a marathon." I think the better metaphor is that it is an ultra-marathon, 100-mile trail run through the mountains, with bears and briars around every corner. When talking to 100-mile finishers, you'll hear them refer to "pacers" who run alongside them on the trail. It is not the pacer's race to run, but they are helpers who come alongside the participant and offer encouragement, nourishment, and protection from the treacherous terrain and elements. These helpers guide the participant on the course and ultimately enable the runner to finish the race well.

Discipleship, as God intended it, cannot happen outside of community. We are not meant to trek this journey in isolation. Just like 100-milers need pacers, your discipleship journey needs community—but not just any community. There must be two things present: Jesus and each other.

Read Matthew 18:20. Discipleship assumes community. However, in this verse, Jesus defines His picture of community: us and Him. Let's unpack that verse. Jesus says, "When two or more are gathered..." That's pretty simple, right? When you're with someone, you're in community. But what follows is the kicker, "...are gathered in my name." Discipleship is communal, but not all community is discipleship. Jesus must be the focus of our community in order to grow in discipleship. Don't confuse fellowship or simply "hanging out" with discipleship. Jesus requires a certain level of intentionality that centers the purpose of gathering with each other around Himself.

The last part is the best; Jesus declares that He will be present with us when the community is focused on Him: "there I am with them." Jesus desires to be in community with us. He wants to be with us on this journey to offer encouragement, nourishment, and protection. But, He also wants us to run alongside each other in a discipleship community to offer the same.

Are you committed to Christ-centered community, or are you just committed to community? Have you made an intentional effort to be a part of a close network designed to bring you closer to Jesus, or are you more committed to building your community focused on sports, fishing, poker, or golf? If the latter is true, now is the time to start investing in life-giving relationships that bring you closer to Jesus.

# DISCIPLE-SHAPING QUESTIONS

1. You are likely already engaged in some type of community. But is that community focused on Jesus? How can you shift the focus of your current community toward one that is Christ-centered?

2. Do you need a new community? Maybe God is using this time to pull you away from relationships that don't draw you closer to Him. Take a few moments and evaluate your community. Write one word that each of your group of friends is focused on. If the focus is not Jesus, prayerfully consider why you're committed to those relationships.

3. Do you have a "pacer" in your life who is willing to run alongside you to offer encouragement, nourishment, and protection in a Christ-centered relationship? Write that man's name down and pray for him right now.

4. Are you currently discipling someone? Ask God to make you the man that he can use to spur along your brothers in Christ.

# WEEK 6 DAY 2

SCRIPTURE PASSAGE: ACTS 2:42-47

In Peter Wohlleben's book, *The Hidden Life of Trees*, he argues that trees, yes trees, are social and thrive in community. As a forester in Germany, he's conducted fascinating research that supports this claim. In one instance, he recalls stumbling upon "stones" in the middle of a beech forest. However, these were not "stones" at all, but the stumps of beech trees that were still living hundreds of years after being felled. How were they still living? He found that the surrounding trees had stretched out their roots and were feeding this aged stump with nutrients of their own in order to keep it alive.

Wohlleben's answer to why this happened is important for us to apply to our study on community within discipleship. He says that one tree on its own cannot "establish a consistent local climate." And in fact, many will die when planted outside of the protection of the canopy. But together, many trees create a forest, and a forest can create an ecosystem that can weather storms and extreme temperatures. But for this to happen, he says, "the community must remain intact no matter what."

That was the posture of the early church as well. Read Acts 2:42-47. The strength of the church and the fulfillment of God's mission depended on each person's commitment to seeking the Holy Spirit's guidance and keeping the community intact no matter what. The Acts 2 community was centered on sound doctrinal teaching, but equally important was their commitment to fellowshipping with one another, eating meals together, and praying together. While no one is asking you to sell all your belongings and live in a commune, the essence behind Luke's words in vs. 45 is that the community's health was more important than the needs of the individual. When the community was healthy, the individual's needs were cared for. As disciples of Christ, we should look to the needs of others and not just our own. Finally, we read that the early Christians opened their homes and shared meals with glad hearts. It's not a coincidence that God added to their numbers daily.

If your idea of discipleship is limited to something that only happens in Sunday school or a church building, then you misunderstand the fullness of community where God blessed and grew His early church. Don't hear that incorrectly; learning about God's word in Sunday school or small group is vital, just as it was for the church of Acts. But limiting your discipleship to Bible study only limits the richness God offers to those within your community. Let's not neglect the community aspect of discipleship that extends outside the walls of your church and into your daily life

# DISCIPLE-SHAPING QUESTIONS

1. Many times, men see discipleship as only teaching and learning about the Bible, but it is so much more than that. There are spiritual conversations and important relationship-building opportunities that happen when we fellowship, share meals, and pray together. How are you actively creating space in your life to facilitate this level of community interaction?

2. In your experience, what has your discipleship community included? Was it only teaching and learning about the Bible? Or did it include an element of fellowship and serving one another as well?

3. What percentage would you say was placed on each of the following aspects of Christ-centered community in your past discipleship experiences?
   a. Bible study:
   b. Fellowship:
   c. Sharing meals:
   d. Prayer:

4. What do you think a healthy community of discipleship should look like based on percentages? No wrong answers here. The importance is that you become intentional about including all aspects of these rich elements of community in your discipleship.
   a. Bible study:
   b. Fellowship:
   c. Sharing meals:
   d. Prayer:

# WEEK 6 DAY 3

SCRIPTURE PASSAGE: HEBREWS 10:19-25

Have you ever considered community as a spiritual discipline? Because Jesus has saved us, we should be assured of our salvation, bold in our faith, and committed to community. Our commitment to community is a response to our salvation through Jesus and a discipline that must be practiced.

Read Hebrews 10:19-25. Pay particular attention to verses 24-25. When we commit to Christ-centered community, we are obeying God's desire for our lives. We were not meant to live our Christian lives outside of community. When we view community as a spiritual discipline, we place greater importance on its value and carve out intentional space where community can happen. Our motives for engaging in community shift from self-serving to Christ-centered. We no longer can avoid community because we "don't feel like it," or "it's just not for me." Community becomes something we do in response to God and not something we use to seek personal gain. When we commit to building community with other believers for discipleship, we fulfill God's desire for our lives.

But why does God desire a commitment to community? Read 1 Peter 5:8. "Be alert and of sober mind. Your enemy the devil prowls around like a roaring lion looking for someone to devour." If you've ever watched a lion stalking his prey, you've noticed a couple of tendencies. Lions don't attack the group; they seek prey that has strayed away from the pack, the ones on the fringe. Lions also don't attack the strong; they attack the weak. And many times, those are the ones who have separated themselves from the strength of the pack.

When believers neglect meeting together and do not commit to community for discipleship, they open themselves to the attacks of the devil—they become weak, vulnerable, easy targets. You've seen it before: a man stops coming to church, stops attending Bible study, and removes himself from a discipleship group. The next thing you know, he's cheated on his wife or made a terrible decision that has destroyed his family. It's much more difficult for a man to fall victim to these snares when he's committed to a discipleship community. God desires a commitment to community for our protection and growth and, ultimately, a life that brings Him glory. Are you seeking Christ-centered community, or are you finding yourself closer to the fringe these days?

# DISCIPLE-SHAPING QUESTIONS

1. Stop right now and pray for a man you know who has fallen to the fringe. This man might have been a regular small group attender, or perhaps he was in your Bible study but has suddenly stopped coming and removed himself from Christ-centered community.

2. Now that you've identified this man, write down three things you are actively going to do this week to reach out to him. Call him, email him, text him, stop by his office, invite him over for a burger, whatever you do, do not lose this sense of urgency. His life and family might very well be depending on you to help restore him to the pack.

3. To practice the discipline of community in your own life, you've got to stop making excuses. Circle the excuse(s) you're most likely to use to avoid community or abuse community.

   I don't have the time.
   I don't get anything out of it.
   I like to be by myself.
   I'll do it only if I'm the leader.
   I don't go because my kids don't like it.
   My kids have sports at that time.

4. Now, reflect on the excuse(s) you circled. How can you fight these lies the next time Satan tries to tell you community is not worth the effort?

5. For men striving to be disciples, community is more than just fellowship. It's more than just friendship. It's hard, messy work at times. But it's God's plan. Pray today and ask God to show you where you can take your community to the next level.

# WEEK 6 DAY 4

SCRIPTURE PASSAGE: GALATIANS 6:1-3

In J.R.R. Tolkien's beloved trilogy, *The Lord of the Rings,* a Hobbit named Frodo Baggins undertakes a quest to destroy the powerful and dangerous One Ring by throwing it into the fiery pit of Mount Doom. Samwise (Sam) Gamgee, Frodo's best friend, and co-adventurer on this quest, noticed the toil the ring was taking on Frodo and how the burden of carrying the ring was making Frodo physically unable to continue. Sam couldn't carry the ring—that was Frodo's task. However, Sam was there to assist him along the way. There, on the side of the mountain, where Frodo was content to die and abandon the quest, Sam pled with Frodo, "Come, Mr. Frodo!' he cried. 'I can't carry it for you, but I can carry you." Then, in a dramatic act of brotherly love, Sam holsted Frodo over his shoulder and scaled the mountain to continue their quest of destroying the One Ring together.

Read Galatians 6:1-3. Community within the context of discipleship means carrying your brother's burdens when possible and carrying your brother when it's not. It's walking alongside each other in good times and in bad. It means sticking close by even if your brother is entangled in sin, then accepting the responsibility to restore him to the faith rather than shunning him for his actions. However, just as a fireman is likely to get burned when rescuing someone from a fiery building, we must be careful when helping a brother caught in sin that we do not fall victim to the devil's schemes as well; and don't think it won't or can't happen to you.

None of us are immune to sin. The further you drift from authentic Christ-centered community, the more susceptible you become to thinking that sin isn't that big of a deal. If you think you are above sin, you're setting yourself up for failure. Every man needs to be discipled by other men in authentic Christ-centered community to help do the following: identify sin in their lives, recognize a way to overcome sin, and assist each other along the new path. Don't let your pride get in the way of your brother's obligation to carry your burdens. That's what men are supposed to do for each other. Helping one another is how men show their love and commitment to God.

# DISCIPLE-SHAPING QUESTIONS

1. Men need other men to help identify the sin in their lives. Does your community love you enough to point out the sin you're struggling with but also help you carry that burden until you've overcome it? If not, pray right now that God would reveal a godly man who is not afraid to shoulder the burden of your sin and walk with you to a life devoted to Christ.

2. What does it mean to carry another's burden? Write down three practical ways you and your community can help someone carry the burden of their sin. This may be financial, physical, or a commitment of time.

3. What ways can you guard yourself against falling into temptation when carrying the burdens of another? Write down three things you should do before helping a man struggling with sin.

4. How can you guard against thinking you are immune to sin? What common practices should you start or continue to help fight against this dangerous mentality?

# WEEK 6 DAY 5

In 2014, Psychological Science released a fascinating study about the power of shared experiences. They concluded that regardless of whether the experience was good or bad, it was enhanced by sharing it with someone else. Researchers discovered that the level of perceived enjoyment was higher when people shared a bad event with others than when a good event was experienced alone. It's the same line of thought that propels teams to sign up for events like Eco-Challenge, or how SEALS bond after completing Hell Week, or how the best stories shared around the campfire are not the uneventful happenings of everyday life but the near-death adventures that you and your buddies experienced together. Regardless of the event, life is better together.

Life was not meant to be lived alone. In good times and in bad, God created us for community. In the same way that God is in community within Himself as the Triune God, we were designed for community. It's in our eternal DNA. Community is part of God's design for enjoying the goodness of His creation as well as overcoming the trials and toils that life throws at every one of us. The writer of Ecclesiastes addresses the value of community amidst hardships. Read Ecclesiastes 4:9-12. As we see in this passage, community provides a safety net for believers. This passage in Ecclesiastes is practical, but let's unpack it with a little more applicability. Based on this passage, the benefits of having a community are that together, people accomplish more, a friend or companion will pick you up when you fall, and your community can offer protection against danger. Sounds like a divinely designed plan for discipleship.

As we conclude this week on community, take a minute to evaluate those you've allowed into your circle. Do they help you accomplish the work of Jesus? Can you depend on them to lift you if you fall? Are they looking out for your interests and not just their own, and willing to protect you against dangers you might be blinded to?

When men engage in this type of Christ-centered community, the devil doesn't stand a chance. It's time to drop the whole "lone wolf" schtick; that's not how God designed you. But it takes hard work and commitment and tossing away of all pride to create the authentic community where discipleship can happen. Are you up for the challenge?

# DISCIPLE-SHAPING QUESTIONS

1. What is keeping you from the Christ-centered community that God desires for your life? Write down all the obstacles you can think of that are holding you back.

2. Now, from that list, choose one and write a counter-argument that will help you overcome that obstacle. It doesn't have to be long; take a minute to write down the truth that will help you overcome that lie.

3. How can you be a better member of that community for other men? Are you available? Are you there when men fall or only when they succeed? Are you the one helping your buddy see the sin in his life, or are you too afraid to call him out?

4. In this space below, write down one thing you can do this week to be a better co-disciple within the community God has given you.

# WEEK 7:

## DISCIPLES ENGAGE WITH THEIR SURROUNDINGS

As Christ-followers, we are called to engage with our neighborhood, our community, our country, and the world in the name of Christ. This is the Gospel in action. God expects His men to be involved in compassionate service for the sake of Christ. This is what you may call being "missional," and this is where many churches and Christ-followers shine, mostly through short term missions and community outreach projects.

But engaging with our surroundings goes beyond mission projects. If you want to be the man God has called you to be, engaging with your surroundings means getting to know your neighbors. Yes, it's serving your community, but it's also seeking opportunities to be salt and light in your workplace. Sure, it's meeting the needs of the "least of these" in your city (and all around the world), but it's also seeing yourself as God's ambassador in your everyday life. It's seeing life through the lens of making a difference and doing so in the name of Jesus, for the advancement of His Kingdom, and the glory of His name. This is what it means to engage with your surroundings. And it's a vital aspect of being a disciple of Jesus.

*This week, Lee Moore will help unpack what it means to be a man engaged with his surroundings as a disciple of Christ.*

# WEEK 7 DAY 1

SCRIPTURE PASSAGE: ACTS 1:8

Last words. How intently we listen to them when they are quietly being uttered in a last breath. We cling to every one of these words, don't we? And years later, we often recall and meditate on them in memory of that person. Read Acts 1:8. Here we have Luke's version of Jesus' last words on earth. How important is this single verse and the final command it contains? "You will be my witnesses . . ." One of the most important and biblical ways we witness is through serving. In Matthew, Jesus paints a direct and clear picture that even He came not to be served but to serve. Serving others is a vital aspect of discipleship, one we can't neglect if we want to grow into the men God desires us to be.

How do we serve? We serve by knowingly taking action. For most men, when we talk about serving, the first word that comes to our mind is "project." What kind of service project can we construct to serve others? Cut a widow's grass? Help build a church? Certainly, these are great ways to serve. However, in serving through a "project," you will only be serving a few days a year, here and there. That hardly seems like the totality of what Jesus was commanding us in Acts 1:8. I want us to see serving as intentionally engaging in daily acts with those brought into our path. A way of life, if you will. You see, to serve the way Jesus is talking about causes us to stop and rethink how we serve daily and how we see the people around us.

I was on a mission trip to New York when after a day of feeding the homeless, one of the guys made a powerful statement: "I cannot come back on this trip until I see the homeless in my city as I see them here." Too often, we project our preconceived ideas onto those around us based upon their outward appearance. We are inclined to view individuals in need as lazy, drug addicts, alcoholics, and people who may not deserve our help. To live a life of service, we must begin to see people as God sees them and treat them with the respect and dignity that Jesus has shown us.

# DISCIPLE-SHAPING QUESTIONS

1. How can you begin to live life on a mission to serve others? What changes do you need to ask God to make in your heart before you can begin to serve Him and others as He expects you to?

2. List three ways you can begin to see people around you as God sees them.

3. Where is God calling you to serve? Spend some time in focused prayer, asking God to reveal to you exactly where He wants to use you.

# WEEK 7 DAY 2

From pep-rallies to fiery halftime speeches, our world is full of people and things that attempt to motivate us. As we look at today's verses, we see what motivates Paul.

Read 1 Corinthians 9:19-23. See how clearly Paul communicates what motivates him. Paul lives his life to bring the Gospel to the world around him by serving others. For Paul, this was an expression of his identity as a disciple of Jesus. Based upon Paul's example, we should disciple by serving those around us, no matter our differences, and pointing them to Christ. When Paul speaks about becoming more like others, he wants us to see the people around us and how we should interact with respect and kindness.

A few years ago, I was staying in a hotel in Austin, TX. While riding in an elevator, I found myself having a light conversation with a man and a woman from the hotel staff about their busy days. By every outward appearance, these individuals were very different from me. As the doors opened, I felt the Holy Spirit prompting me to continue interacting with them. We paused in the hallway, and I began to explain to them that even though we have different accents, hair color, and skin color, and that even though they were much younger than me, we are the same in the light of the cross. Each of us needs a Savior. They politely said, "thank you," and continued on their path. As I turned to walk away, I felt disappointed. I don't know what I expected, but the conversation just seemed to not be as meaningful as I hoped.

The next morning at breakfast, the lady from the elevator stopped me. She thanked me for sharing with her and her companion. She said she was a believer and the young man was a Muslim. He only understood a little of what I said, but it opened up the door for her to share the Gospel with him! You see, when we obey the Holy Spirit and see people as important, even though they may be different from us, there will be opportunities to share Christ. We may share His love, or it may open the door for someone else to share His love.

To be a disciple of Christ is to be like Him. Take some time today to ponder how in the Gospels we see Jesus treat others. Then, ask yourself probably the most difficult question of all: how do you treat the outcast and the ones who are not like you?

# DISCIPLE-SHAPING QUESTIONS

1. What inside of you keeps you from engaging people who are different from you?

2. You will never serve others unless you cultivate sincere care for them. What work does the Spirit need to undertake in your life to see your heart transformed? Are you willing to surrender your life to God and allow Him to change your attitudes toward those who are not like you?

3. If you have children, what messages are you sending them about the kind of people you serve and the level of commitment you have in meeting the needs of those less fortunate than yourself?

4. Spend some time in prayer today asking God to help you with your attitude toward others, especially those who may be considered "different" from you. Listen to what God is trying to tell you. Be willing to let Him speak into your life and continue to make you more of a faithful disciple.

# WEEK 7 DAY 3

SCRIPTURE PASSAGE: MATTHEW 5:13-16

Most guys I know like action. From movies to activities, we want to be doing something that motivates us, that's exciting, that gets our adrenaline pumping. Some like extreme thrills, like jumping out of airplanes or climbing Mt. Everest. Others like to hunt, fish, golf, workout, and so on. Men love to be involved in activities that get their adrenaline pumping. Why, then, do we lose this motivational "adrenaline pump" when it is time to serve a lost world that God cares so much about?

Read Matthew 5:13-16. In this passage, Jesus compares His disciples to salt and light. In Biblical days salt was used, among other things, as a preservative to prevent meat from decay. Just as salt preserves meat, Jesus calls us to stop the effects of sin in the world around us. Jesus knew that a little light could light up a hillside. Our lives are to shine a light on a lost and dying world. We tend to shy away from this vigorous discipline of discipleship because it takes us out of our comfort level. It causes us to interact with those we would like to not interact with. How can we become the salt and light to those around us? I think Augustine gives us a great starting point: "Since you cannot do good to all, you are to pay special attention to those who, by the accidents of time, or place, or circumstances, are brought into closer connection with you."

We often fail to do anything because we look at the bigger picture and feel that we cannot make a difference. I encourage you to start the day in prayer not only for your needs but for the needs of others. Not just others you know, but to those you will come in contact with through the "accidents of time, or place, or circumstances." It will require great effort to be aware of the people coming into your life and the opportunities you have to serve and encourage them. It will require you to be intentional every day, from the mom with a buggy full of groceries and four kids clinging to her, to the older man who sits alone at a dinner table. Those are easier to see. Ask yourself the hard question: What about those who are very different from me? Those on the other side of the political spectrum or with different beliefs?

Engaging our surroundings as a disciple of Christ means that we look for ways to serve others regardless of race, sexual preference, or political view. What if they have been brought into your life specifically so they can hear that God loves them? As a disciple of Jesus, we're bound by His love to love and serve others. We will be known as His disciples by the way we love.

# DISCIPLE-SHAPING QUESTIONS

1. Think of three or four ways you've been salt and light to someone in the last few days or weeks. Jot them down in the space below.

2. What triggered your decision to act? What was it that set your service in motion?

3. What will it take for you to take your service to the next level? What actionable steps can you take to see this area of your discipleship grow?

4. Take time today to ask God to reveal to you any blind spots you have when it comes to serving others.

# WEEK 7 DAY 4

SCRIPTURE PASSAGE: ISAIAH 58:6-10

Take a moment and read Isaiah 58:6-10. To a guy who loves double cheese-burgers and chocolate milkshakes, the word "fast" is always a little scary. But we need to realize that in this verse, God is speaking to the condition of our heart while we fast. The Israelites physically fasted, but it was the condition of their hearts that did not please God. It would be like us going to church and tithing on Sunday morning and then going to our favorite restaurant and belittling our waitress at lunch.

Men, today is the day that the rubber hits the road. Serving others should be our natural lifestyle. It requires us to see those around us as God sees them: valuable, important, the one sheep worth leaving the other 99 for. Too often, we see people as groups instead of as individuals when we think about serving.

About a year ago, we moved into a new house in a new city. A neighbor, who is in his 80's, came over and introduced himself. He welcomed us to the neighborhood, gave us some fruit, and invited us to his church. Our house-hold garbage is picked up on Tuesday and Friday of each week. We have a large rolling garbage container that must be taken to the curb for the sanitation workers to empty on those days. Every Tuesday and Friday, before we get home from work, our dear, sweet neighbor has rolled the can back up our long driveway.

Feeling guilty that an 80-year-old man was doing a job that we were physi-cally able to do, I let him know that he didn't need to go out of his way to roll our garbage can back up the driveway. He just looked at me, smiled, and said, "This is the way I show my neighbors I love them." One day we noticed that this neighbor saves his garbage can for last. He purposely goes to each house on our street and rolls their garbage cans to their houses before finishing with his own. There certainly could be many reasons why he chooses to bring his container up last, but we believe it is because he cares about everyone else above himself. He wants to serve others in the way Christ served others.

What deeds of service is God calling you to do for the poor and oppressed? What deeds of service is He calling you to do for your own family? Just as it's hard to think of the Bible without the stories of the woman at the well and the healing of the ten lepers, it's just as hard to think we can claim to be a disciple without caring for the socially outcast and the poor of today.

# DISCIPLE-SHAPING QUESTIONS

1. Ask the question, do we merely claim the title of Christian, or are we a disciple who loves and serves our neighbor?

2. List three opportunities you have to serve the outcast and poor in your community, and when specifically you can carry these out.

3. Take some time to reflect on why you've struggled in the past to serve the poor and the needy in your community. What is it that keeps you from taking action?

# WEEK 7 DAY 5

SCRIPTURE PASSAGE: PHILIPPIANS 2:14-16

Have you ever asked someone to help you do something, and after hearing them complain, you wished that you had just done it yourself? Worse yet, have you ever been asked to attend a dance recital, cheer competition, beauty pageant, or maybe a craft fair with your wife? Even though you said yes, you would rather have been doing something else, and everyone could tell. We have all likely found ourselves doing something for family and friends we were doing with less than a thankful heart.

Read Philippians 2:14-16. The verses here in Philippians have more to do with our hearts toward serving others. We could probably stop after the first five words of the verse and have years of self-correction to work on. Do all things without grumbling. Serve our families without grumbling. Serve the people in our lives without grumbling. Go to work without grumbling. No Grumbling. Zero none. Wow. Why? So that we might show that we are born again children of God! Jesus knows firsthand that serving others is difficult. We understand that we live in a crooked and perverse generation, but we fail to realize that this does not excuse us from serving.

As you wrap up this week on service, my prayer for you is that your light shines by your acts of love and service and that you would not run or labor in vain. How horrible it would be to get to the end of our lives and look back only to discover that everything we did was for our attention and glory, and none of it mattered for the Kingdom of God. Men, our heart matters. Let us begin to serve the King of Kings by serving others with a thankful heart, and may that heart be filled with the love of God.

One of my favorite Leonard Ravenhill quotes speaks to our hearts when it comes to service: "There are three persons living in each of us: the one we think we are, the one other people think we are, and the one God knows we are!" Who are you more concerned with? Only you can answer this question. Are you a disciple who loves and serves others with a thankful and joyful heart? Are we running the race to show the love of Christ for our glory? Let us not be deceived into thinking we can use the word disciple and not love and serve others.

# DISCIPLE-SHAPING QUESTIONS

1. List three ways your attitude toward serving can improve.

2. Have you ever been guilty of serving only for the attention? If so, write out a few occasions of when and how.

3. Is it your heart's deepest desire to finish the race strong and not in vain? If so, how do you believe God would have you accomplish this?

# DISCIPLES INVEST IN MULTIPLYING DISCIPLES

There is a powerful truth about the Gospel: it compels itself to be heard. Its power can't be contained. When the Gospel takes hold of our lives, we're changed. For some, it's a first-time introduction to a relationship with Christ. For others, a deeper commitment to the Gospel leads them to a deeper commitment to Christ. Regardless of where an individual is in this spectrum, as men seeking to be more faithful disciples, we must be a part of this Gospel multiplication.

There are two types of multiplication that we want to see men involved in, Kingdom multiplication and individual multiplication. *Kingdom multiplication* is evangelism. It's the Gospel shared in word. Though we can never limit the Spirit's ability to spontaneously lead people to salvation, the most effective evangelism men can embrace is "life-on-life." This kind of multiplication is personal. It's grace driven. It's godly men seeking out the lost in their sphere of influence and inviting them into their lives to see how Christ has rescued them. It's Kingdom multiplication one person at a time.

Individual multiplication is the expectation that as men committed to following Christ, we will be shepherding younger Christ-followers. As men mature in their faith journey, they are called to be traveling along with others. The wisdom these men have based on their time walking with God is to be imparted to others to help their growth. And as these other, younger followers grow, the expectation is that they would, in turn, engage in multiplying their followership through someone else.

*In this final week, TJ Gilliam will show you that to be a faithful disciple, you must invest in multiplying disciples.*

# WEEK 8 DAY 1

SCRIPTURE PASSAGE: MATTHEW 16:24-26

I remember the first time I heard the words from my football coach, "It's not about you." It struck me as harsh because I had built my whole persona around myself. If I wanted to win, which I did at all cost, I had to put down my ego for the whole team to succeed together. This realization was not easy because, like most men, I was stubborn. (To be honest, I still am at times.) But this truth stuck with me long after my playing days were over. It's a truth that can also be applied to our discipleship journeys. When we make our journey about ourselves, we miss out on all the best things the Lord has for us, the most important one being Himself.

Do you consider yourself to be a high achiever or goal-oriented person? Do you like to have control of your circumstances or situation at all times? Do you like to create opportunities based on your preferred outcome? In today's culture, we are taught that we are the only one who is "for us," and as long as we do what's best for us, we will be successful. The world gives us a false sense of identity. In our passage today, Jesus shatters that narrative.

Read Matthew 16:24-26. Jesus told His disciples, "If anyone would come after me, let him deny himself." To follow Jesus means to completely surrender all of you and embrace all of Him. He calls us to surrender our will, our wants, and our ways, to trust in His will, His want, and His way. He calls us not to merely surrender part of our lives; that doesn't take much faith. He is calling us to "all-in" surrender. It's you exclaiming, "Lord, I hand it all to you. Everything." It's quite a bit to consider.

Jesus knows that this is a deep decision for us. He further says that if we attempt to save our life, we will lose it. Why? He knows that we can never be satisfied with what this world has to offer. It will always leave us empty and wanting more of whatever the next "thing" is. The Lord knows we are prone to chase after temporary things, and He gives us a warning that we lose our soul in this pursuit. We grow more distant from Him the more we choose to pursue the gains of the world.

There is hope! Jesus tells us we can find true life and true profit in Him! We often look at the cost of following Jesus and think of all that we may have to give up or lose, but it is time to change that mindset. Think of what and who you gain! You gain true life in the Savior, Jesus. You gain so much more than you will ever lose. He is worth it all.

# DISCIPLE-SHAPING QUESTIONS

1.When you read Jesus say that we are to deny ourselves, or an old coach's challenge, "It's not about you," what challenges immediately came to your mind? Why do we as men struggle with denying ourselves?

2.With what are you trying to fill your life in an effort to preserve or save it? What would you do if it was all stripped away from you? Is Jesus enough for you? Be honest and write in your thoughts below.

3. It is wise to count the cost of any decision. Jesus is giving us the cost in our verses today. Read them one more time. When you read this deep call of discipleship, do you dread more of what you may lose? Or do you grow in gratitude of all you will gain? Spend some time below writing all the things you gain when you go all-in on being a disciple of Christ.

4. Spend some time in prayer today. Ask the Lord to help you see what it is that you are still withholding from Him. Ask Him to help you understand that the more of ourselves we lay down, the more of Him we receive. Ask the Lord to teach you to be satisfied in Him and Him alone.

# WEEK 8 DAY 2

SCRIPTURE PASSAGE: MARK 1:16-18

We are all on a journey. Inevitably, on your life's journey, you have had a moment where someone showed you how to accomplish a task or work more effectively. We all have those moments. We have had those men who have spoken spiritual truths into us. We have had those that have disciplined us, encouraged us, or pushed us beyond where we thought we could go. When we look at the influence Jesus had on His followers, He did all of this and more.

Read Mark 1:16-18. The first thing we must see in this passage is that Jesus is on a journey. He is on the go and calling others. As disciples, we should pattern ourselves after the model Jesus gave us. To begin making disciples, you must first check to make sure that you are on a journey. Are you seeking after the Lord with your heart, soul, mind, and strength (Mark 12:30)? Are you seeking and setting your eyes on the things that are above where Christ is (Col. 3:1-2)? Are you pursuing the denial of self in order to know the fullness of Christ's life for you (Matt. 16:24-26)? Your journey is significant. You will only be able to take others where you have been. Men, to disciple, you must be a constant disciple yourself.

As Jesus was passing along the Sea of Galilee, He saw Simon and Andrew. It is so significant that Jesus notices ordinary people and speaks to them. He saw these two fishermen and engaged them in their arena. As disciples, we should keep our eyes open and looking toward the others we pass by on our daily journey. The Lord places people in our lives on purpose. Just as Jesus did, we should notice and engage them. It may be uncomfortable or even awkward at first, but Jesus gives us this model of discipleship.

Jesus doesn't want people to just be fans of Him when He calls them. He calls them to something with a deeper purpose. As we are on our journey with the Lord and begin to notice other men, we should be inviting them to join us on a deeper journey with Him. We should be actively looking for other men to join us in our discipleship journey as we seek to follow God together.

It is important to note that Simon and Andrew immediately left their nets and followed Jesus. Others will want to follow when there is something worth following. As you begin to seek out others to disciple, remember that you are not just inviting them to follow you, but you, like Paul, can say, "follow me, as I follow Christ."

# DISCIPLE-SHAPING QUESTIONS

1. Think back over your life and identify the people that have discipled you. Did you have a pastor, a small group leader, a friend, or a mentor that encouraged you in your walk with the Lord? Write their names below and write one specific thing they did that led you to pursue the Lord more.

2. Let's take a quick inventory of how you are doing in your pursuit of the Lord. Are you seeking after the Lord with your heart, soul, mind, and strength (Mark 12:30)? Are you seeking and setting your eyes on the things that are above where Christ is (Col. 3:1-2)? Are you pursuing the denial of self in order to know the fullness of Christ's life for you (Matt. 16:24-26)? Consider these questions and spend time asking the Lord to reveal to you His truth and to cover you with grace.

3. On your journey, who are you passing often or each day that you should be inviting into a discipleship journey? What is stopping you from engaging them?

4. Here are two challenges for you today. First, contact one or two of the people that you listed that pushed you to pursue Christ more to simply tell them "thank you." Second, commit to the Lord to inviting one person to begin a discipleship journey with you.

# WEEK 8 DAY 3

SCRIPTURE PASSAGE: MATTHEW 28:19-20

Our lives are full of choices. We're surrounded by options. Let's take shoes, for example, specifically Jordans. Jordans have long been the most iconic athletic shoe named after, arguably, the greatest basketball player of all time, Michael Jordan. The Jordan brand of shoes expanded year after year while MJ was playing and continues to this day. If you go into a shoe store that carries the shoe line, you will find what seems to be endless options of styles and color combinations. It can get overwhelming and expensive very quickly.

Read Matthew 28:19-20. Jesus' command to "go therefore and make disciples" is not a simple suggestion, passing thought, or an option. This is an imperative that we are to follow. This is Jesus' command to multiply and grow the Kingdom through evangelism. No one can call themselves a disciple of Jesus and neglect His call to evangelism. There are many ways you can go about it, but what must be settled in your core is that, as you seek Christ, you are called to lead others to Him also.

Jesus' command for us to "go" was a mandate to go and make disciples "of all the nations." This is a massive calling over our lives that can feel overwhelming. Like all the options we have in front of us every day, this can feel like just another choice. The beauty of this calling is that, although it is large, it's also very personal. To make disciples, to baptize and teach them, it requires proximity to those who have been reached. Often the greatest tool of evangelism is "real life" proximity. Who works next to you? Who is your next-door neighbor? Who is in your hobby circle? Who is in your influence circle?

The command to "go" is one you have likely heard before. Whether you are well seasoned or completely new to evangelism, the call is the same and the power of Christ being "with you always" remains true. Men, it is the telling of "Christ in you, the hope of glory" (Colossians 1:27) that brings hope of eternal life in Christ. There are options for telling of this hope, but being obedient to the call is not one of them. Making disciples is a command from the Lord and is our opportunity to join in reaching the nations in the name of Christ, one person at a time.

# DISCIPLE-SHAPING QUESTIONS

1. In your lifetime, have you treated Matthew 28:19-20 more as an option rather than a command? Do you personally struggle with personal evangelism? Why do you think that is?

2. The Gospel is the same, but the way we go about sharing it can differ for every person. If you could describe the best scenario that would allow you to be comfortable sharing the Gospel with someone, what would it be? Describe it below. After you write it down, pray that the Lord would provide this scenario for you in the next week.

3. "Life proximity" is often our greatest tool of evangelism. Think about the people you regularly encounter: your neighbor, co-worker, influence circle, friend group, etc. Do you know if they are disciples of Jesus? Who do you need to commit to starting a conversation with about the Good News of Jesus? Write their names below and commit to the Lord that as He provides opportunities, you would be obedient and share.

4. The Lord wants to see the people of the Kingdom multiplied, and He desires to use you to do it! Jesus promises to be with you, always. How does knowing this encourage you or calm your spirit when it comes to evangelism? How does reading and counting it as truth in you push you to get started?

# WEEK 8 DAY 4

If you have ever been on any kind of team, you know that each person has a defined position or area of expertise. This is because of their specific skillset or strengths in a specific area. In a work environment, the goal is to get the best person to fill the company's available positions because it will make it more efficient and effective. You can go back to elementary days when two team captains would choose their teams. They would alternate picks. Whether you were the first or last pick, you had a role to play on the team. Why? Because the captains chose you to be a part of the team.

This is true in the Kingdom of God, as well. The Lord has chosen us in adoption as sons. Furthermore, through the indwelling of the Holy Spirit, you have been equipped and called off the sidelines of life and have been directly placed on the team. There's no more space for sitting on the sideline and observing. You have a role to play, and it is an important one!

Read Ephesians 4:11-16. In our passage today, we see Paul laying out the importance of investing our lives in disciple-making by defining various roles to the church at Ephesus. As he did to the Ephesian Christians, Paul calls us to equip the saints. Who are the saints? Our spiritual brothers and sisters. We are to invest in or equip them so they can be effective in ministry, strong in faith, and a part of seeing the Body of Christ grow.

Men, if you are a follower of Christ, you have been gifted by the Holy Spirit. I believe that the Bible is clear that it is a sin to neglect that gift and neglect our spiritual family. When we do not embrace our gifting and live out our calling as mature, godly men, it affects the entire body of Christ.

We all have a role to play. We are not called to sit on the sidelines. We are called to invest ourselves in the work of leading others to grow closer to Christ.

# DISCIPLE-SHAPING QUESTIONS

1. Read Ephesians 4:11-16 one more time. You need to accept the call to make disciples of others. List below three to five reasons for spending your life pouring into other believers.

2. You have a major role to play in the Kingdom when it comes to evangelism and discipleship. There truly isn't a greater investment of your life than leading others to a closer walk with the Lord. Have you been neglecting your gifting when it comes to discipling others in one or more areas? How could you begin multiplying your discipleship those people in your home, church, and community? Why do you think this is?

3. Spend some time praying today. Pray that the Lord would reveal to you any areas in your life where you are sitting on the sidelines of discipleship. Pray that He would lead you to both pursue Him and actively pursue ways to equip the saints.

# WEEK 8 DAY 5

Have you ever been injured and needed help? Maybe you had a simple cut but needed help finding a bandage. Or maybe you had a major injury and needed help getting to the emergency room. When my daughter was born, she was incredibly ill, and we had to fly her from one city to another for the proper medical care. The doctors' knowledge of the right procedures and medicines was so incredibly calming to my wife and me. The nurses and assistant staff were so helpful. Ultimately, my daughter's little body was healed, and she was able to come home. I have often wondered, "What if there were no doctors or medical schools to train medical personnel? Would my daughter be alive?" It causes me to stop and be thankful for all the Lord has done.

Think about your spiritual journey. Who was there to bring the Good News to you? Who led you closer to the Lord? Who has poured into you over time? Have you ever stopped to think that whoever those people are, they were sent by God and were obedient in their call to share Jesus with you?

Read Romans 10:9-15. There is power in the Good News. The Gospel is the life-giving story of Jesus' mission of love and life. And we have the responsibility to carry it to the lost. Just as a medical team works with all their might to make sick people well, we should give all we have to see those dead in sin become alive in Christ! There is a power contained in verses 14-15 that should cause you to stand up and thank God for calling you. Men, as disciples of Christ, we are to go and to share the Gospel as often as possible and with whoever will listen. You see, Paul wrote how one comes to following Jesus in Romans 10:9-13. But verses 14-15 describes who was to go and tell. That's you! God's plan is to use His people to see His Kingdom multiplied. Now, it's your turn to go and preach so that all may hear, so that all may believe!

# DISCIPLE-SHAPING QUESTIONS

1. Read Romans 10:14-15 again. Paul is following up verses 9-13 with intense passion. You can feel the tone when you read it. When you read this, what do you feel? How does that align with what you believe?

2. With this passage and this weeks' devotionals, we can see that God desires for you to be a disciple that makes disciples. Someone brought the Good News of Jesus to you. Now it is your turn to take it to them. What, if anything, at this point, would cause you to not go and tell? Would you lay it before Jesus here in our last day together?

3. We are called into this incredible work of reaching the nations. Why do you think Paul calls the feet of those who preach the good news "beautiful"? In what ways does this encourage you?

4. God gave us a life that has been made new. Paul gave us the words to say. Jesus commissioned us to go and tell. Today, spend time praying that the Lord uses you to multiply the Kingdom through discipleship and evangelism.

### ANDY BLANKS
Chapter 1: Disciples have been transformed by Christ

Andy Blanks is the Publisher and Co-Founder of YM360 and Iron Hill Press. A former Marine, Andy has been in the ministry since the early 2000s, mostly in publishing and discipleship. During that time, Andy has led the development of some of the most popular Bible study curriculum and discipleship resources in the country. He has authored numerous books, Bible studies, and articles and regularly speaks at events and conferences, both for adults and teenagers. He is active in his local church, teaching youth, adult, and men's small groups. Andy and his wife, Brendt, were married in 2000 and have lived in Birmingham, AL, ever since. They have four children, three girls, and one boy.

### RICH WINGO
Chapter 2: Disciples surrender to a Gospel-centered life

Rich Wingo is originally from Elkhart, IN, and was recruited by Coach Paul "Bear" Bryant to play football for the University of Alabama (1974-1978). Rich was part of the famous "Goal Line Stand" in the 1978 Sugar Bowl, where Alabama won the National Championship. After graduating, Rich played for the Green Bay Packers for seven years. After his decorated professional football career, Rich coached at The University of Alabama (1987-1989) before serving as President of AIG Baker Real Estate (1990 - 2010). He is Senior Director of Development at Blackwater Resources in Birmingham, AL, and a member of the Alabama House of Representatives (Republican District 62). Rich is married to his wife of 41 years, Cheri. They have two sons, two daughters-in-law, and four grandchildren.

### CHAD POE
Chapter 3: Disciples hunger to know God

Chad Poe is originally from Chattanooga, TN. He is a graduate of the University of Tennessee at Chattanooga, where he received a Bachelor's Degree in Secondary Education. Following college, he attended Southwestern Seminary in Fort Worth, TX, where he received his Master of Divinity. After graduating seminary, God called Chad to a life of itinerant ministry. Chad teaches Scripture through storytelling, media, and visual experience. As a result, the Bible is clearly presented for people of all ages to examine and apply Biblical truth to their everyday walks of life. Chad and his wife, Hope, live in Lake Jackson, TX, with their three sons and a daughter, where he serves as Teaching Pastor at Grace Bible Church. He is an avid reader and an infrequent visitor to the gym.

### ERIC BALLARD
Chapter 4: Disciples desire to worship God

Eric Ballard is an author who has written Bible studies, devotionals, books, and Christian curriculum for Union Gospel Press, Lifeway, The Youth Cartel, YouthMinistry360, Downloadable Youth Ministry, Likemind, Zaner-Bloser, and Manhood Journey. He calls Texas home, where he lives with his beautiful wife and two daughters. Before getting his master's at New Orleans Seminary, Eric graduated from the prestigious Mississippi State University, where he spent many years chasing intramural sports championships. Because of an illustrious soccer career that was cut too short, most nights, Eric still sits by the phone waiting for the Houston Dynamo to finally call him up.

## RICK BURGESS
Chapter 5: Disciples pursue personal holiness

Rick Burgess is the Co-Host of the nationally syndicated Rick and Bubba Show. He has co-authored multiple New York Times Bestselling Books covering topics such as politics, marriage, business, comedy, and what it looks like to be a follower of Christ in secular entertainment. Rick has appeared on the Fox News programs Hannity's America, Your World with Neil Cavuto, and Fox and Friends. He regularly speaks at men's events and marriage conferences across the country and teaches a weekly Bible study. Rick is married to the former Sherri Bodine, and they have five children: Brandi, Blake, Brooks, Brody, and Bronner. Rick's wife Sherri is the author of the book "Bronner: A Journey to Understand," a powerful story about what she and Rick learned about God through the earthly death of their youngest son, Bronner. Rick's eulogy for Bronner became the most-viewed video in the world on YouTube the week of the service.

## BRYAN GILL
Chapter 6: Disciples embrace Christian community

Dr. Bryan Gill has worked in higher education for over 15 years and is currently an administrator and instructor at Samford University in Birmingham, Alabama. After earning his bachelor's degree from Auburn University, he attended Beeson Divinity School, where he earned his Master of Divinity, then later received his Doctor of Ministry from Gateway Seminary of the Southern Baptist Convention in California. He has authored or contributed to numerous books and articles focused on bringing people closer to Jesus. He is currently the men's minister at his home church, Shades Mountain Baptist, in Birmingham, AL. Bryan enjoys all things outdoors, especially fly fishing and wildlife photography, and is co-host of The Storied Outdoors podcast. He and his wife, Sarah, have been married since 2006, and they have two children.

## LEE MOORE
Chapter 7: Disciples engage with their surroundings.

Lee Moore has been actively involved in the ministry for decades. Since 2013, Lee has served as the Director of Customer Care for YM360, where he leads out in serving youth workers in the local church. He also plays a similar role for Iron Hill Press and The Man Church, consulting with men's ministries interested in implementing discipleship strategies. Lee currently serves as the Character Coach of Lawson State Community College Baseball and routinely speaks and preaches in churches and Christian organizations. Lee and his wife, Tammy, live in Birmingham, AL. They have four children and seven grandchildren.

## TJ GILLIAM
Chapter 8: Disciples invest in multiplying disciples

TJ Gilliam grew up in rural Little Rock, AR. He has been married to his high school sweetheart, Melanie, for 18 years and has one middle schooler and one high schooler. While in college at Arkansas Tech University, TJ met Jesus at 20-years-old and has never been the same. He was a student pastor for 15 years in Arkansas and Tennessee before joining Strength to Stand (a student conference, camp, and tour ministry in Birmingham, AL). He also served as the Directional Pastor for Christ City Church. TJ has spoken in churches, camps, conferences, retreats, Firefighter schools, school systems, and events around the country and internationally. He is currently on staff at Mission of Hope as part of the Church Partner Engagement Team. He has a passion for sharing the Gospel and making disciples everywhere he goes.

# HOW DO YOU BECOME A MAN?
## *BY LIVING LIKE JESUS*

*How To Be A Man: Pursuing Christ-centered Masculinity*
is a 40-day devotional experience that will challenge you to a more passionate
pursuit of growing in to the man God is calling you to be.

Using 8 core characteristics, this devotional experience will challenge you to exemplify
these in your own life as you passionately pursue a Christ-centered manhood.

- Identity
- Integrity
- Purpose
- Surrender
- Passion
- Commitment
- Compassion
- Influence

SAMPLE ONLINE AT IRONHILLPRESS.COM/PURSUING

# GOD GAVE US THE STORIES OF *REAL MEN* TO TEACH US WHAT IT MEANS TO FOLLOW HIM.

*How To Be A Man: Learning From the Real Men of the Bible* is a 40-day devotional that examines the lives of eight men from the Bible. Using their lives as an example, men will be challenged to live a life of impact and influence, changing the world around them for the sake of the Gospel.

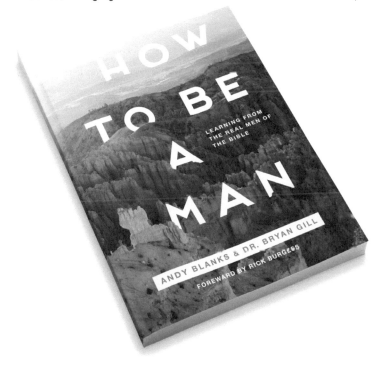

The men we meet in the pages of the Bible are real people. And we can learn much from them, men like:

- Abraham
- Joseph
- Joshua
- David
- Elijah
- John the Baptist
- Peter
- Paul

TO SAMPLE & ORDER, GO TO IRONHILLPRESS.COM/REAL–MEN

# IRON HILL

*press*

---

Iron Hill Press is a collective of people who love Jesus, love Gospel truth, and love sharing those things with others through the medium of publishing and Gospel-centered event experiences. Learn more about us at ironhillpress.com.